Document Style Guide

for Oil Companies and Contractors

by
LORI JO OSWALD, PH.D.
Wordsworth LLC

ISBN-13: 978-1505442410

ISBN-10: 1505442419

Publisher: Wordsworth LLC Publishing

PO Box 2397, Palmer, AK 99645

www.wordsworthwriting.net

To contact the author or publisher, e-mail: editor@wordsworthwriting.net

WORDSWORTH

Writing, Editing, & Document Formatting Svcs.

Words worth writing are ... words worth writing well.
Wordsworth ...
because your words are worth it.

TIPS FOR USING

Thank you for purchasing Wordsworth LLC's Style Guide for professional firms. This has been designed specifically for oil companies and their contractors but may be useful to other professional firms as well as individual writers.

This can be a useful training tool. The first six chapters can be assigned to personnel to read (it may take 2 to 3 hours); the rest can be used for reference on an as-needed basis.

If you would like to order a Microsoft Word version of this document to personalize it for your company, just order from our Web sites, either wordsworthwriting.net or formsinword.com. You may wish to substitute (or add to) your own acronym list, your own references style, your own font style, or your own sample documents. There are sections that are "rules" that should stay the same, and then there is a section titled Company Style, which can be changed.

I would like this to be a document that makes your job easier as well as makes the company look better, so your input is welcome and encouraged. If you have any questions or suggestions related to this style guide, I will be glad to answer them at no extra charge. Just e-mail your questions to us at editor@wordsworthwriting.net.

Our documents tell our clients a lot about us, and they should be error-free; it is therefore essential that you allow time for every document to be reviewed before it goes out. Thank you for caring about your company's words, style, and presentation!

Sincerely,
Lori Jo Oswald, Ph.D., Author
Owner, Wordsworth LLC

ACKNOWLEDGMENTS

I am grateful to the many technical editing clients I have worked with over the last 20 years.

For sources, I have used and highly recommend *Merriam-Webster's Collegiate Dictionary* and the *Chicago Manual of Style*. There are many other excellent references out there, but these are my two favorites.

Thank you to Eva Nagy, my assistant editor, for her suggestions on this document.

TABLE OF CONTENTS

LIST OF TABLES AND FIGURES

TABLES

FIGURES

1.0   INTRODUCTION

The purpose of this style guide is to provide writing tips, editing guidelines, and samples for your company. But this style guide has other functions as well. I have included specific acronym and style lists to help make report writing and editing at your company easier.

Consider this a guide in helping you through the writing or editing process. It is subject to change, and you are encouraged to add your suggestions and changes and give them to the technical editor for inclusion in future versions of this document.

Another element of this guide, and one which you might find slightly confusing, is that I have written it so that it not only guides you but also can *become* your own company style guide. (A Microsoft Word version can be purchased online at wordsworthwriting.net or formsinword.com if you wish to have it in Word for ease of adding your company's name and other personalizing touches.)

Why is a style guide important? The answers are consistency, clarity, and professionalism. Every document—e-mail, memo, letter, proposal, or report—gives an impression to clients or prospective clients about our company. As one editor said, "What we sell are reports." One mistake, such as writing 2.5 liters instead of .25 liters, can have serious consequences as well as make us seem unprofessional. Errors distract from messages, cause credibility problems, and can communicate the wrong information. Our clients expect and demand high-quality writing.

Do we expect you to catch every error or check for every possible item mentioned in this guide? Definitely not—this is mostly a reference manual and will mainly be used by the technical editor. There is no such thing as a perfect draft. The writer handles the prewriting and writing stages, while the technical editor edits and proofreads the document. Peer reviewers can also serve as helpful editors. This guide has sections for both writers and editors.

Editing and writing are different tasks and require different people to do them. All good writers have editors. When an editor makes changes, corrections, and suggestions on a copy, there is nothing personal intended toward the writer. This is simply a common—and important—

step in creating a strong, clear, and clean document.

Please don't let fear of your high school English teacher's red pen prevent you from passing on your company documentation to an editor. The editor does not judge you personally, talk about you, or think you are less of a person because your document has mistakes.

I will tell you an editor's secret: We love mistakes. We love finding and fixing them. We love thinking about words and the best ways they can be used to accomplish the assigned task. Additionally, a document with mistakes in it is much more interesting to read than a near-perfect one. And never once, in nearly 30 years of editing, have I thought poorly of an author because of the document I was reading. I think only of the words themselves, the purpose of the document as a whole, and the intended audience.

Most important is that the writer—and the company in general—knows that each document—no matter how small—should go through a review process, including the technical editor and at least one peer. Reviewers need to edit for the following:

- Grammar, punctuation, and spelling
- Style and format
- Organization and logical presentation
- Readability and appropriateness to the intended audience
- Inclusion of all required elements (i.e., Executive Summary, List of Acronyms and Abbreviations, References, etc.)
- Consistency and accuracy of data in the text, figures, and tables
- Figures, Tables, and References (text locations and consistent format)

There are many resources to help with writing and editing, in addition to this guide. An English handbook, such as those required in college English classes, is useful. I also rely on *Merriam-Webster's New Collegiate Dictionary* for final decisions about spelling, capitalization, and hyphenation. Another important source for editors, and for some of the information in this style guide, is the *Chicago Manual of Style*. It is an excellent, detailed manual that you should add to your library.

2.0   DOCUMENT REVIEW POLICY

As part of your company's commitment to quality control, all documents should go through the following review process (this may be different at your company):

- The initial document (or revision) is prepared by at least one employee, who then sends it to the technical editor.

- The author then submits the document to one or more qualified peers or supervisors. The reviewer keeps track changes on so that the author and technical editor can review those changes.

- The peer reviewer sends the document back to the author for revisions.

- The document is reviewed by a technical editor, who edits for grammar, content, organization, style, and formatting.

- The editor's changes are reviewed by the author. Track changes are accepted and comments are addressed and deleted, unless the author wants the peer reviewer to see them. Track changes for new sections or author changes are turned back on, so the editor can review these changes in the final version.

- The final version is e-mailed back to the technical editor who checks the changes by the author and peer reviewer and submits the document back to the author.

- The document is approved by a senior manager.

Since writing and editing are different processes requiring different skills, it is strongly recommended that all document writers obtain at least one edit from someone else.

Even formal letters and memos should be reviewed by someone other than the author. Proposals, letter reports, and draft and final reports should all be read—at a minimum—by a peer reviewer, a technical editor, and a senior reviewer.

Figure 2-1 shows the editing review process I recommend. Of course, not all companies can afford this complete process every time, but I hope if I convince you of nothing else in this manual, it is that a technical editor is an essential element in quality control. Your company will be presented to your clients as more professional, and you will reduce or eliminate risk in making embarrassing mistakes (often I have found inaccuracies in table or figure data and the text, for example).

All writers, including editors who write manuals, need an editor.

Figure 2-1   Document Review Flowchart

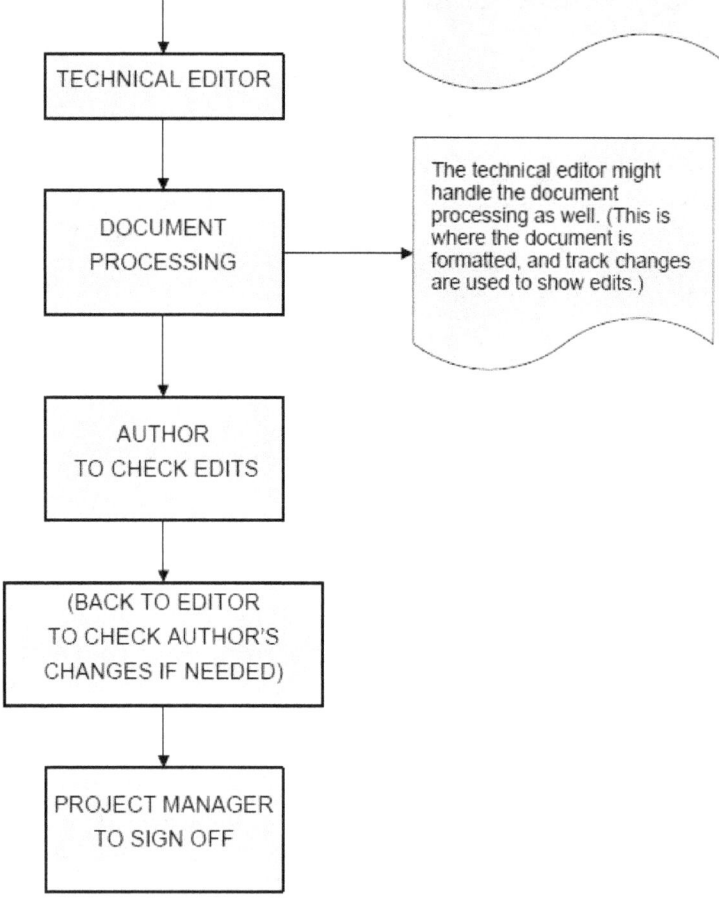

2.1   Peer Review

Peer and senior edits are made to evaluate the concepts and conclusions from a technical standpoint, as well as to provide any other feedback as needed. Remember, the more readers your document has before it goes to the client, the better!

2.2   Technical Editing

The technical editor, or someone else qualified to edit the report, should edit the document in the following areas:

- Evaluating grammar, punctuation, spelling, house style, and format (using this style guide as a source);

- Checking the organization of sections within the document, as well as the overall document;

- Looking for conciseness and readability;

- Making sure there is consistency among and within the text, tables, and figures;

- Determining whether there is a logical and clear progression from findings to conclusions; and

- Looking for the presence in the text of all the required sections.

Here are some specific areas the technical editor should check for in each document:

- Figures, graphs, and tables are clear;

- Data in text match data in tables, numbers in tables and figures are correct;

- Figures and tables are referred to in the text; figures and tables either directly follow the first textual reference, or are located on the next page following the first textual reference;

- An acronym (and abbreviation) list is included;

- Each acronym is defined the first time (and only the first time) it is used in the regular text (exceptions: Transmittal Letter, Executive Summary, figures and tables, and resumes are treated as separate documents);

- The use and capitalization of acronyms are correct (per the acronym list in this style guide);

- Font size and style are correct;

- References are in proper company format;

- Bullets are used instead of numbers with lists, unless numbers represent sequential steps;

- The use of *and/or* is avoided if possible;

- Appendices are referenced in order in the text and are complete;

- Maps are clear, legible, and checked for spelling;

- The text is not too technical-sounding or filled with jargon or vague phrases;

- Title page has proper elements, including the client's name and address, project number, and date;

- Table of Contents matches text, including page numbering, headings, appendices, and titles of tables and figures;

- Transmittal letter and executive summary are edited;

- The headings are worded properly to reflect the text that follows;

- There are enough headings; and

- The numbering and font styles of the headings are appropriate.

It is also important that the technical editor, the original writer, or a peer check the document after it is returned from document processing to be sure all changes were made correctly and that the formatting is still correct.

Try to understand the time needed by the technical editor to do a thorough edit. Although many reports require little editing (rewriting) but instead require mostly proofreading (fixing errors in grammar, punctuation, and style), the average time involved in technical editing is six pages per hour, which means a medium-length report will require at least 6 to 12 hours to complete. Figures and tables often add more time. Also, remember that the editor probably has other documents to complete before yours. Try not to say, "Just do a quick edit," to the editor. There is no good way to do that. You would be asking for a shoddy, incomplete job.

2.3   Document Processing (or Formatting)

The document processor puts the document in the proper format (i.e., report, proposal, letter, memo) using the appropriate fonts, margins, headings, footings, etc., according to the specifications in this style guide, unless other specifications are given by the author or technical editor.

The document processor also does the following:

- Adds the Table of Contents page
- Inserts tables and figures and the correctly formatted table and figure headings (using the "Captions" feature in Microsoft Word)
- Inserts page breaks
- Inserts page numbers

Nowadays, the technical editor often performs the Document Processing duties since documents are usually edited in Microsoft Word, on a computer. Some editors still prefer to mark up the hard copy; this can allow for a more careful, if slower, read, and if the company affords it and the editor prefers it, wonderful! Most of my clients are rushed, especially regarding proposals, and I am expected to do it all and quickly.

3.0 PUNCTUATION ("THE RULES")

This section lists common punctuation rules and errors with examples similar to the ones we encounter in your company's documents.

3.1 Apostrophes

- Apostrophes are not used for plural forms of years and acronyms: 1990s, USTs.

- Apostrophes are used to show possession. The apostrophe precedes the "s" when the noun is singular; it follows the "s" when the noun is plural. There is no need for a second "s" after the apostrophe. Examples: the client's bill, the USEPA's decision, Robert Edwards' letter, your company's documents.

- Its and it's are often confused; *its* is the possessive form, and *it's* is a contraction for *it is*. Examples: The agency believed its decision was correct. It's not important to me. (Do not use it's in technical writing; see next bullet item.)

- Do not use contractions: it's, can't, don't, won't, wouldn't, etc.

3.2 Capitalization

- Generally, we tend to use capitals unnecessarily. If you are not sure, you probably do not need to capitalize the word. To be sure, you can use *Merriam-Webster's New Collegiate Dictionary*; if it is capitalized there, go ahead and capitalize it. Also, follow the guidelines in this section.

- Acronyms and abbreviations are usually in all capital letters, although the words they are based on are often not capitalized. To be sure, check the abbreviations and acronyms list in Section 13.0 of this style guide. Example: inside diameter variation (IDV).

- Capitalize titles only when they directly precede a person's name or are part of an address: The source of the information was Project Manager Jane Szmanski. The project manager is Jane Szmanski. Jane Szmanski, project manager, is. . . .

- Generally, capitalize counties, states, municipalities, cities, and boroughs when they are part of a name. They are usually lowercased when they precede a name: Kansas City, the Municipality of Anchorage, the state of Alaska, the city of Palmer, Washington State, the Pacific Northwest (the proper name of a region), northern Washington (a general direction).

- If you are referring to a specific document, table, entity, or organization, capitalize it. If not, lowercase: draft reports, *Draft Report 1 for Bethel Landfill*, Figure 1-5; the figure; the Environmental Services Agency; the agency; the Federal Bureau of Standards; federal, state, municipal, and city agencies; the federal Department of Transportation; the federal government; Congress and the Senate; the state senate and the state legislature; the department; the Department of Public Works.

- Do not capitalize "the" before a company or institution name: the University of Alaska Anchorage.

- Capitalize the first word in columns and bullet lists if each item is a complete sentence or is particularly lengthy. For simple words or short phrases that finish the sentence preceding the bullet list, lowercase the individual bullet items, use commas or semicolons at the end of each item as is appropriate, and end the final list item with a period. For example:

  The ground is

  - hard,

  - cold, and

  - dark.

- Capitalize specific geographic names but not general terms: John, Paul, and Mary creeks, Yukon River, the lakes, Lake Ontario, lakes Stephan and Willamette, Winston Lake.

3.3   Colons

- Colons are often used to precede lists. They are also used to precede clauses or phrases that clarify or illustrate.

- Use only one space after a colon (and after a semicolon, for that matter). The contractor discovered three flaws: first, a loose bolt; second, a missing nut; and third, a broken screw.

- Colons in text are used after complete sentences (i.e., you should be able to replace the colon with a period). The same rule should apply to colons before bullet lists (but we are flexible here and allow for an incomplete sentence before a bullet list if necessary). Examples: We have six requests: the first . . . , the second . . . , etc. Bring four items to the campsite: food, bedding, equipment, and bear spray.

- In the text, do not use a colon after the word "includes" or "including" unless the words "the following" appear after. Example: The punctuation list includes commas, semicolons, and periods. The list includes the following: cheese, bread, and water. It is acceptable to use a colon after "includes" or "including" before a bullet list, but it is still preferable to have a complete sentence before any colon.

- Although you usually need a complete sentence before a colon, you do not need one after a colon. However, it is not wrong to have a complete sentence after a colon. Examples: I have six pets: two dogs, two cats, and two horses. The monitoring well data were incomplete: additional testing was required. (Note: The writer could have used a semicolon, a period, or a comma with a conjunction [and] instead of a colon in the last sentence.)

- Use a colon after a salutation in a letter instead of a comma (Dear Mr. Jones:).

- A colon can be used after one word, as we have been using throughout this document with the word "Example." Example: This is such a case. For example: Here is another one.

- When the expressions namely, for instance, for example, or that is are used in a sentence to introduce a list, a comma is usually used instead of a colon. Example: Birch's study included the three most critical areas, namely, McBurney Point, Rockland, and Effingham.

3.4　Commas

Comma rules can be confusing, so we have provided subheadings for each use to help you find the appropriate rule quickly.

3.4.1   *Using Commas in a Series*

Always use a comma before "and" or "or" in a series of three or more items. This is a style requirement, not a rule. You might notice that most newspapers use Associated Press (AP) style, which does not use the last comma in a series. Most magazines use the *Chicago Manual of Style*, which does require it. It is standard in formal writing to use the comma. For example:

- Mammals in Area A include caribou, fox, and lemmings; mammals in Area B include polar bear, walrus, and several species of whales and seals.

- It was a fast, simple, and inexpensive process.

Incorrect in Technical Writing: The corporation requires its employees to be loyal, hard working and prepared.

Correction: The corporation requires its employees to be loyal, hard working, and prepared.

When adjectives modifying the same noun can be reversed and make sense, or when they can be separated by either "and" or "or," they should be separated by commas:

- The drawing was of a modern, sleek, swept-wing airplane.

But when an adjective modifies a phrase, no comma is needed, as in the following example, where *damaged* modifies *radar beacon system*.

- The company investigated the damaged radar beacon system.

If there are only two items in a series, no comma is necessary.

- The drawing was of a modern sleek airplane.

3.4.2   *Using Commas to Separate Complete Sentences*

If you have two independent clauses (i.e., complete sentences that could stand on their own) separated by a coordinating conjunction (and, but, for, or, so, yet), put a comma before the coordinating conjunction. If the second clause is not an independent clause, do not use the comma before the coordinating conjunction.

- The pack ice breaks off from shore ice in June, and the shore is free of ice from late July until mid-August.

- The Gubik formation is mainly of marine origin and consists of lenses of gravel, sand, silt, and clay.

3.4.3   Using Commas to Set off Phrases (Which, That, Who)

Usually, when you use the relative pronoun "which," you have a phrase that needs to be set off from the rest of the sentence with two commas. Usually when "that" is used, there are no commas. Whether or not to use commas before and after a clause beginning with "who" depends on the meaning of the sentence. If the information following the word "who" is essential to the meaning of the sentence, do not use commas; if it can be eliminated without changing the meaning of the sentence, do use commas.

- The company's new style guide, which will be in use by December 1, ensures consistency in all documents.

- The style guide that the company is presently using is outdated.

- The editor, who studied at the University of Washington, is based in the Fresno office.

- The editor who is the most skilled in that area is in the Palmer office.

3.4.4   Using Commas with Names, Titles, and Addresses

Commas are used to separate distinct items in the text. Therefore, if you write an address on one line, separate the elements in this way: Chris Polsky, 4117 Ravensdale Road, Seattle, Washington. Note that the state is spelled out in the text, but in letters and addresses, use the postal code abbreviation (listed in Section 13.0, Abbreviations and Acronyms):

> Chris Polsky
> 4117 Ravensdale Road
> Seattle, WA 97506
> (206) 777-7677
>
> Dear Chris Polsky:

Note that in the salutation, above, a colon is used instead of a comma in formal writing. Also, I addressed "Chris Polsky" instead of "Mr." or "Ms." Polsky because I am not sure whether Chris is a man or a woman, based on the name.

Here are some additional uses of commas with names, titles, and addresses:

- Toronto, Ontario, Canada

- Sally Jo Rogers, Ph.D.

- John Smith, P.E.

- LMB, Inc.

3.4.5 Using Commas in Numbers

Use a comma in numbers larger than 999: 131,000, 9,000, 800.

3.4.6 Using Commas after Introductory Phrases

In technical writing, always use a comma after an introductory phrase, in order to avoid confusion. For example, notice how the comma clarifies this confusing sentence: To be successful managers with MBAs must continue to learn. Revised: To be successful, managers with MBAs must continue to learn.

3.4.7 Using Commas with Quotation Marks

Commas and periods always go inside the closing quotation marks; semicolons and colons always go outside closing quotation marks.

- Smith said, "I didn't do it," after he saw me.

- I said, "Yes, you did."

- I don't know why he said he "didn't"; it was clear that he did.

3.4.8 Using Commas in Dates

- August 27, 1999, was the day he proposed.

- The subcontractor conducted the site assessment in June 1998.

3.5 Dangling and Misplaced Modifiers

Dangling modifiers can be tricky to spot, but the rewards are worth it. A dangling modifier is a word or phrase that modifies a word which does not appear in the sentence (or is in the wrong part of a sentence). Here are some examples (the first two are from grammar.about.com):

- Sipping cocktails on the balcony, the moon looked magnificent. (This sounds like the moon drinks.)

- Exhausted after the long hike, the shady hammock was a welcome sight. (How can a hammock be exhausted?)

- After looking behind the garbage container, the polar bear was located.

Spotting these can be challenging, but fixing them is easy. Add in the subject. For the third bullet item above, for example, add the missing subject after the comma: After looking behind the garbage container, the scientist found the polar bear.

Here are some more humorous examples from eddiesnipes.com:

- While reading the newspaper, the cat jumped on the table.

- The young girl was walking the dog in a short skirt.

- The dog was chasing the boy with the spiked collar.

- The hunter crouched behind a tree waiting for a bear to come along with a bow and arrow.

- The woman walked the dog in purple suede cowboy boots.

- We saw dinosaurs on a field trip to the natural history museum.

- Hopping briskly through the vegetable garden, I saw a toad.

3.6   Dashes

Dashes come in three lengths: hyphens (-) (which are discussed in Section 3.9), en dashes (–), and em dashes (—).

3.6.1   En Dashes

- Our company's style is generally to have one space around en dashes. En dashes are the shorter dash.

- Microsoft Word will automatically change a hyphen to an en dash as you type, as long as you have the space before and after the hyphen.

3.6.2 Em Dashes

- Dashes are usually used to emphasize the text in between them—to tell the reader this is important and look here—so they should be used sparingly.

- Dashes can also be used to define words. Anorexia nervosa—an eating disorder characterized by an aversion to eating and an obsession with losing weight—is common among young female gymnasts and ballet dancers.

- Type two hyphens with no spaces around them, and Microsoft Word should automatically replace them with a dash.

- There are no spaces around em dashes.

3.7 Ellipses

Ellipsis points (plural: ellipses) are a set of three or four spaced dots (periods on the keyboard) showing missing text from quotations. Usually you can quote without having to resort to using them (as in the first example below), but here are some ways they are used.

- Example without ellipsis: Peter Singer said that stones "do not have interests" because they can't suffer, while a mouse does have "an interest in not being kicked down the road, because it will suffer if it is" (1975).

- Quotation with ellipsis: Yi-Fu Taun, author *of Dominance and Affection: The Making of Pets*, said that the breeding process is used to make animals more useful or desirable for humans: "With the horse . . . humans have tried to make the animal both larger and smaller" (1984).

- Use a fourth "dot"—a sentence-ending period—along with the ellipsis points when an ellipsis comes at the end of your sentence or when the material you have deleted contains at least one period: Summer also said that people have described personal space as "a small shell, a soap bubble, an aura. . . ." In *Animal Liberation*, Peter Singer wrote, "Nearly all the external signs which lead us to infer pain in other humans can be seen in other species. . . . Behavioral signs—writhing, facial contortions, moaning, yelping or other forms of calling, attempts to avoid the source of pain, appearance of fear at the prospect of its repetition, and so on—are present" (1975).

- Note spacing requirements: with three "dots," space before and after each one; with four dots, do not space before the first one (or after the last one if a quotation mark immediately follows it).

- The ellipsis points should not be separated at the end of a line and into the following line. This can be a problem in right-justified text. You may have to revise your sentence to fix it.

3.8 Exclamation Points

- Avoid! Avoid! Avoid! They do not belong in formal writing! In fact, most good writers don't use them at all, except perhaps in a quotation! (Jane screamed, "Eeek!") And especially never use more than one!! That would be most inappropriate!!!!!!!

3.9 Hyphenation

- Hyphens connect related items, often modifiers that precede a noun (tie-in, toll-free call, two-thirds, one-year-old child).

- Hyphens are often used unnecessarily after prefixes. Check the lists in *Merriam-Webster's New Collegiate Dictionary* if in doubt. (To save time, nowadays I go to www.m-w.com and just type in the words I need to check there.)

- Here are some examples of words that do *not* take hyphens after the prefixes: preexisting, semivolatile, nonprofit, nonhazardous, nonnegotiable. See Table 3-1 for a list of prefixes that do not usually take a hyphen (always confirm at www.m-w.com or in your Merriam-Webster's dictionary if you can).

- For the examples in which *Chicago Manual of Style* does not take a hyphen but Merriam-Webster's does (e.g., coworker or co-worker and prolife or pro-life), I usually go with Merriam-Webster's dictionary. It is my "go-to" source for capitalization, hyphens, and spelling. I have included, in this manual, a list of commonly used (and confused) words; I use them exactly as in that list.

Table 3-1   Prefixes Not Requiring Hyphens

Prefix	Example	Exception
after	aftereffect	
anti	antisocial	
bi	bilingual	

Prefix	Example	Exception
co	coworker	*Note: Merriam-Webster's does use a hyphen with most co- words.*
counter	counterbalance	
equi	equilibrium	
extra	extracurricular	
infra	infrared	
inter	interstimulus	
intra	intraspecific	
macro	macrocosm	
mega	megawatt	
meta	metacognitive	meta-analysis
micro	microorganism	
mid	midterm	
mini	minisession	
multi	multiphase	
non	nonsignificant	non-achievement-oriented students
over	overaggressive	
post	posttest	*I know it looks like "post" should take a hyphen, but check the list in Webster's (or m-w.com); it rarely does. Still, if a company insists or its style guide demands, I will not argue, and I will use the hyphen.*
pre	preexperimental	pre-1970, pre-UAA trial
pro	prowar	*Note: Merriam-Webster's does use hyphens with most "pro-" words.*
pseudo	pseudoscience	
re	reevaluate	re-pair (pair again), re-form (form again)
semi	semidarkness	
socio	socioeconomic	
sub	subtest	
super	superordinate	
supra	supraliminal	
ultra	ultrahigh	
un	unbiased	un-ionized (not ionized)
under	underdeveloped	

Source: *Chicago Manual of Style*

- Exceptions to the above include the following: if the prefix stands alone (pre- and postclosure elements), if the root word is capitalized (mid-August, non-American), if the root is a number (pre-1900), if the resulting word can have two meanings (retreat and re-treat or un-ionized and unionized), or if the second element consists of more than one word (non-English-speaking, non-achievement-oriented students).

- Generally, hyphenate words with the prefixes ex, all, and self and the suffix elect: all-encompassing, self-employed, president-elect.

- Hyphenate a numeral and a unit of measure used as an adjective: three 1,000-gallon tanks; 3-, 4-, and 6-inch-diameter pipes.

- Do not use a hyphen after adverbs ending in –ly: previously installed wells.

- Do not hyphenate Latin terms: in situ (per Webster's; you will see this term handled differently by different companies and agencies however, so if a client prefers another way—hyphenated or italicized or both—go ahead and use that style for that client.

- Hyphenate two words of equal value used as modifiers: gray-brown soil.

- Hyphenate compound modifiers when one word modifies or defines another but does not separately define the noun being referred to: dark-green building (but no hyphen in large green building, since large does not modify green).

- Before a noun, hyphenate a compound consisting of a noun and a participle: decision-making skills, broad-based experience. But do not hyphenate if the expression follows the noun: Her experience is broad based. The well is 73 feet deep.

- Hyphenate a phrase used as an adjective before a noun (up-to-date account) but not if it follows the noun (the account was up to date).

- Hyphenate compounds containing numbers that precede the noun: 23-year-old woman, twentieth-century innovation, one-year program, 7-foot depth, 7-foot-wide opening. But there is no hyphen in the following: in three years, 35 gallons of fuel, the woman was 23 years old.

- Hyphenate fractions that are spelled out: one-half, two-thirds.

- Hyphenate when referring to specific figures and tables: Figure 4-1, Table 3-7.

- Although most of the time numerals 10 and over are not spelled out, if you must begin a sentence with a compound number, do spell out and use a hyphen: forty-six, one hundred sixty-three.

3.10   Parentheses and Brackets

Generally, try not to overuse parentheses. Some editors believe that if it is not important enough to include as part of the text, then delete it. If it is important, set it off with commas or dashes instead. But, of course, sometimes it is necessary or useful to include parenthetical expressions. So here are some tips to guide you:

- Periods go inside parentheses when a complete sentence is contained within the parentheses. (We have tentatively scheduled this meeting for June 16, 2001.) Otherwise, put the period outside the parentheses: Previous studies found the landfill area safe (Compton, 1989).

- No other punctuation mark should directly precede the first parenthesis mark. The findings were explained by Smith (1989), and they were confirmed by Jones (1993).

- Within a parenthetical phrase, if you have another parenthetical phase, use brackets: Buck (in *The Call of the Wild* [1903] by Jack London) was one of the most developed dog characters in literature.

- However, for code regulations that already contain parentheses, use brackets on the outside where you would normally use parentheses: [24 CFR 1600(4)(5)].

3.11   Quotation Marks

- Quotation marks are used only around direct quotes (i.e., words taken from a source exactly as they were written). If you are changing or condensing the information from another source, still give credit, but do not use quotation marks. The latter is an indirect quote.

- Direct Quote, Complete Sentence: John Smith said, "This is wrong."

- Direct Quote, Word or Phrase Only: Darrell Cohen said he is "positive" the actions were appropriate.

- Direct Quote, Word or Phrases with Material Deleted: According to Daniel Danielson, the site was "always empty . . . and left alone."

- Direct Quote, Complete Except Material Deleted from End of Sentence: Patricia Meyers said, "I don't think I can agree with that assessment. . . ."

- Direct Quote, Material Missing from Beginning of Quoted Sentence: Hillary Capra said that the area "is in need of a bulldozer and explosives." (Note: There are no ellipses marks used at the beginning of a partial quotation; the word "that" preceding the quote as well as the lower case "is" tell the reader that this is not a complete quotation.)

- Indirect Quote: John Smith said that he disagrees with Mark Benson on the results.

- Periods and commas always go inside quotation marks: John Smith said, "I don't think so," and Jane Doe said, "I agree."

- Colons and semicolons always go outside quotation marks: John Smith said he is firmly "committed"; his partner is undecided.

- Single quotation marks are used only within double quotation marks: John Smith said, "James told me, 'I am sure,' before he left."

- When quotations are longer than four lines or 40 words, remove the quotation marks, introduce the quotation, and set the direct quotation off with two indents, as in the following example (for readability, we have indented this example more than 10 spaces or 2 tabs, so that you can see the indent easier in this bulleted section). In *Handbook of Technical Writing*, Alread, Brusaw, and Oliu (2000) explained how to set off quotations:

> Material that is four lines or longer (MLA) or at least 40 words (APA) is usually inset; that is, it is set off from the

body of the text by being indented from the left margin ten spaces (MLA) or five to seven spaces (APA). The quoted passage is spaced the same as the surrounding text and is not enclosed in quotation marks. . . . If you are not following a specific style manual, you may block indent 10 spaces from both the right and left margins for reports and other documents.

3.12   Semicolons

Everyone should have a favorite punctuation mark, in my view. Mine is the semicolon. But semicolons are only used in two ways.

- The first and the most common is between two independent clauses not joined by a conjunction (examples of conjunctions include *and, or, for, so, but, yet*): I am right; you are wrong.

  Often, these sentences contain a transition word or phrase such as *however, furthermore, for example, consequently*, or *moreover*. The semicolon precedes the transitional word or phrase as long as there is a complete sentence both before and after it: I believe I am right; however, I am open to suggestions. I do not, however, agree. (Note that there is a comma after the transitional word when a semicolon precedes it.)

- The second use of the semicolon is to clarify a list that contains commas. The semicolon separates elements that go together. For example: I have lived in Anchorage, Alaska; Eugene, Oregon; New York, New York; and Seattle, Washington.

4.0 COMPANY STYLE

This section lists our "house style" for document text issues. Many of these items are not necessarily "rules" of grammar or punctuation. Instead, the word "style" refers to a company's preferences for how such items as acronyms, commas in a series, capitalization, justification, and italics are used.

There are almost as many styles as there are companies and publications. Newspapers, for example, usually use the Associated Press (AP) style. The styles I have chosen for this style guide is based on standards in the technical writing industry, the *Chicago Manual of Style,* and the Government Printing Office style, as well as the preferences of our clients. These are subject to change. However, it is important to be consistent within documents themselves, and within our company. Therefore, try to follow these style guidelines when writing your document. The technical editor will also look to make sure that all documents meet our style requirements; therefore, do not worry if you are not sure of something or do not have time to check everything. This is the editor's job, and this section is mainly written for editors and document processors to use. This is probably the most important section of this style guide, as it sets down the guidelines for our own company's style.

4.1 Abbreviations and Acronyms

- There is no need to use an abbreviation if a term is only used once. Just spell out the term. (Example: The U.S. Environmental Protection Agency is . . .)

- If using an abbreviation more than once, place it in parentheses after the complete term first appears. From then on, use the abbreviation only. (Example: The U.S. Environmental Protection Agency (USEPA) is . . . According to the USEPA . . .)

- Generally, do not use "the" before abbreviations (example: TPH was detected). Exceptions are certain government agencies (the USEPA, the ADEC).

- Abbreviations and acronyms are generally treated as singular nouns (the USEPA is the agency overseeing the program). Make acronyms plural by adding s (no apostrophe), as in VOCs. Only use the apostrophe for possession (the FDA's position).

- TPH and BTEX are collective nouns that take singular verbs; do not add the "s" to them: Total petroleum hydrocarbons were detected; TPH was detected.

- Do not define U.S., Latin abbreviations (etc.), or compass directions (NE). Some companies prefer not to define F (for Fahrenheit) or C (for Celsius) as well. Abbreviations do not contain periods, except U.S., in., Mr., Ms., no. (number), p. (page), pp. (pages), Latin abbreviations (i.e., et al., etc., e.g.), and degrees (Ph.D., M.A., B.S.).

- Some companies and agencies capitalize all words in their acronyms list, but I do not. I follow the correct capitalization for that term. For example, I capitalize Quality Assurance Plan (QAP) when it is referring to a specific company plan but not when it is referring to such plans in general (QAP is all caps in either case, of course).

- The original words that the acronym represents are not necessarily capitalized; see the abbreviations and acronyms list in Section 13.0 of this document to be sure. (Example: method reporting limit [MRL]).

- Articles agree with the pronunciation of the acronym: an MSDS (em ess dee ess), a RCRA assessment (rik-rah).

- Latin (i.e., e.g., etc.). You do not need to define Latin abbreviations. But do make sure you are using them correctly. i.e. means that is, e.g. means for example, and etc. means and so forth or and so on. Check Merriam-Webster's Tenth New Collegiate Dictionary if you are not sure of the meaning of a Latin abbreviation (see the abbreviations section near the back of the dictionary).

- Always use a comma after i.e. and e.g. Also, they should be used in parenthetical text only: The tanks hold two liquids (i.e., gasoline and methanol).

- If etc. ends a sentence, do not add a second period. Usually you can avoid using etc. by revising the text to include a phrase such as "and others" or "and so on." Another way is to revise the phrase that precedes a list by adding the word includes or including. Instead of writing *The mammals I saw were moose, elk, rabbits, etc.* write *The mammals I saw included moose, elk, and rabbits.*

- Treat résumés, executive summaries, transmittal letters, and figures and tables as separate documents. Redefine acronyms and abbreviations in them. Provide a key to all acronyms and abbreviations used in the tables and figures; the key goes at the bottom of the table or figure.

Section 13.0 contains lists of commonly used acronyms and abbreviations in this field. However, you may find that some have changed or that your company has others to add to this list. If searching on the Internet for the correct spelling, capitalization, and usage of an acronym or abbreviation, I prefer to find government agency Web sites for sources. You will find many errors online, of course, and it may take some searching to find a reliable source. By including the acronyms and abbreviations sections in this document, I hope to have saved you time.

4.2   Companies and Agencies

- Use the name as the company or agency does on its official documents. It may contain and, &, Inc., Co., or Company.

- You can shorten Company to Co. and Incorporated to Inc.

- Usually there is a comma before "Inc.," but if the company is not using a comma in its official documents, leave it out.

- A company is singular, so it takes a singular verb. Also, if you use a pronoun to reference the company, use "it" instead of "they."

  <u>Example</u>: Champion Word Services is skilled in providing detailed editing to corporate documents. It is also . . .

  Since the word "it" is a bit awkward sounding, this is a good place to use an acronym [CWS] as long as it is defined previously; to use "The company"; to use the company's full name again; or to combine the two sentences and eliminate the need for the subject to be repeated (e.g., Champion Word Services is skilled in providing detailed editing of corporate documents and in providing quality workshops to corporate personnel).

4.3   Company, Software, and Equipment Names

As a technical editor, you will find it useful to keep lists of items you use frequently in documents, including the following:

- acronyms and abbreviations;

- previous projects (with exact titles);

- company names (including subcontractors that you might use in proposals, for example);

- software titles; and

- equipment (again, you might list these in proposals).

Although I have included an acronyms list at the end of this document, company names are so numerous and varied that it will be necessary to create your own.

I often see inconsistency in company and product names in documents, which is why I added this section. Specific inconsistencies are seen in capitalization, spelling, and spacing of equipment and software names. The purpose of this list is to provide an accurate, exact list of all of company, software, and equipment names; keep the list updated; and avoid confusion and inconsistencies in your documents.

Below, I have provided some examples from company, software, and equipment based on hydrographic surveying, for an example of what you might create for your own company.

4.3.1   Company Names Examples

The following company spellings, for example, including capitalization, spelling, hyphenation, were checked on company Web sites. Whenever possible, I included in my list the company Web site address for checking additional products, updating names, and other questions.

Triton Elics International (can use Triton or TEI for multiple uses; just define first use)

Products:

BathyPro™

Bathy+Plus™

DelphMap™

DelphNav™

Delph Seismic®+Plus
HydroSuite™
Isis® Sonar
SeaClass™
SGIS™
Thales GeoSolutions Group Ltd.
Thales Geosolutions (Pacific) Inc.
Trimble®

4.3.2 Equipment Names

These equipment names have been taken directly from company Web sites, so the spacing, spelling, capitalization, and the use of the TM or R symbols should be correct. Whenever possible, I have inserted the company (manufacturer's) name in parentheses after the equipment or software name. The rule on the ™ or ® symbol is to either use the symbol throughout the document or to use it at least the first time the product is mentioned in a document (the company would no doubt prefer the first technique, but for proposals, I usually use the second; for published reports, I use the first [i.e., list TM or R symbol with every mention]).

AutoCAD
AutoCAD/MAP
Bathy+Plus™ (Triton Elics International)
BathyPro™ (Triton Elics International)
CARIS®
CARIS® HIPS
CARIS® SIPS
Delph Seismic®+Plus (Triton Elics International)
DelphMap™ (Triton Elics International)
DelphNav™ (Triton Elics International)
Echotrac (use Odom Echotrac)
ESRI
HydroBat (Reson software)
HydroSuite™ (Triton Elics International)
HYPACK®
HYPACK® MAX
Isis® (side-scan sonar acquisition system made by Triton Elics International)

Isis® Sonar (Triton Elics International)

MapInfo

MicroStation (made by Bentley Systems Inc.)

Morad Electronics Corp. (manufacturer of antennas)

Odom

Odom Echotrac (a dual-frequency survey echo sounder)

ORE Offshore

ORE Offshore Trackpoint (Be specific: Trackpoint 4440A or Trackpoint II; give full name if possible)

Polaris Imaging

Polaris Imaging EOSCAN® (a sonar data acquisition and display system)

Reson (full name of U.S. company: Reson Inc.)

SeaBat (Reson software)

SeaClass™ (Triton Elics International)

Seapath 200 (made by Seatex Inc.)

SGISTM (Triton Elics International)

Tripod Data Systems (a Trimble® company)

Triton Elics International (can use Triton or TEI for multiple uses; just define first use)

Triton Isis®

WaterLOG®

WinFrog (Thales Geosolutions)

4.4   Dates

- Do not add letters to a date: June 27, not June 27th.

- Do not shorten: 1970s, not '70s

- Use a comma with month, day, and year: August 18, 1999, was the date of the test.

- Do not abbreviate months in text (okay in figures and tables): December, not Dec.

- Only use an apostrophe with a date if it is possessive. Examples: The 1990s were very good years. In my experience, 1974's best song was "Me and Mrs. Jones."

4.5 Headings and Titles

- Capitalize the first word, the major parts of speech (nouns, adjectives, adverbs, and verbs), other parts of speech with four or more letters (including prepositions with four or more letters), and the last word in all levels of headings: Memory in Hearing-Impaired Children, On-Site Wells, Playing With Fire.

- Do not use 0.0, 0.1, 0.2, etc. as a chapter heading. The first chapter should begin with "1," as in 1.0, 1.1, 1.2, etc. The Transmittal Letter, the Abbreviations and Acronym List, and the Executive Summary do not have heading numbers.

- The following are the fonts normally used in standard company reports. You do not need to format the fonts; they are provided here for your information. The technical editor or document processer will take care of this. You also should never number your headings; this is automatically done by document processing using the styles feature in Microsoft Word.

  - Caps, Centered, bold, Arial 14, *number at left is 4.0*

  - All caps, left justified, bold, Arial 12, *number at left is 4.1*

  - Upper and lowercase, left, bold, Arial 11, *number at left is 4.1.1*

  - Upper and lowercase, number is indented .5 (1 tab), no bold, italic, Arial 10, *number at left is 4.1.1.1*

  - Fifth-level heading. Italics, Arial 10, underlined, *do not use number at left*

4.5.1 Heading Introductions

Always write at least a one-sentence introduction under a heading title before going on to another heading title. For example: This section describes the 2002 remediation activities at the Bethel Landfill.

4.6 Italics

- Generally, avoid italics in formal writing, except for the following examples.

  - Italicize the names of vessels: the *Exxon Valdez*.

- — Italicize the taxonomic names of genera, species, and varieties: The mountain is covered by second-growth forests of Douglas fir (*Pseudotsuga menziesii*).

- — Italicize foreign words and phrases only if they have not yet entered common usage (do not italicize in situ; this is commonly used).

- — In the text and in the reference list, italicize titles of major documents; do not use quotation marks around such titles: *Final Report: Bethel Landfill Cleanup.* When you refer to chapters or articles within larger works (such as an article within a journal), use quotation marks around the shorter work's title: In "The Story of the Essay," from Jane Doe's *English Secrets*, we learn that every successful essay has a thesis. Do not put quotation marks around section titles of reports, however. Example: Section 1.0 of this document contains an overview of the work performed.

- Do not italicize punctuation that precedes or follows italicized words or sections.

- Do not italicize punctuation before or after an italicized word, just those that are part of the italicized material.

4.7   Justification

You have two choices with company style: left justification or full justification. Some believe that full justification looks more professional. Tests reveal that left justification (i.e., ragged right) is more readable, especially with lengthy and technical material. Therefore, it is acceptable to use ragged right in your company documents.

4.8   Lists (Bulleted and Numbered Lists)

Bullet styles vary from company to company and from style book to style book. These are guidelines for our company documents but are always subject to change. For now, these are our preferences.

- Generally, bullets are preferred to numbers for lists. Numbers can be used in sequential steps.

- Perhaps most important is the introductory sentence or phrase to the list. Again, there are lots of styles and discussions on this, but for consistency, the following outlines our company's preferred style. It is up to you, or to the editor, whether to use a colon after the last word preceding the bullet list even though the sentence might be a fragment (e.g., The three tests run were:). If you can make a complete sentence to precede the colon, this is preferred. One way to do this is to add the words "the following" to the clause you have and then use a colon. Example: The methods used will include the following:

- Note that if you use the word "include" or "including" in your introductory sentence, you have an incomplete list following. Drop the "include" if you have a complete list. The animals seen included wolves, moose, and ptarmigan. (Other animals were also seen.) The animals seen were wolves, moose, and ptarmigan. (No other animals were seen.)

- It is important that each bullet item be parallel to the others. Therefore, if one is a complete sentence with a period, the others should all be complete sentences with periods.

- If each bullet item is not a complete sentence, do not use periods. Also, make sure they each follow the introductory sentence (i.e., that they make sense when joined with the introductory sentence).

- If you use commas at the end of the bullet items, add the word "and" after the last comma (i.e., the second to last bullet item), and insert a period at the end of the last bullet item.

- If there are commas within bulleted items, but the entire bullet list is part of a complete sentence, use semicolons instead of commas at the end of each bullet item (and a period at the end).

- Capitalize the first word of each item in a list if each item is a complete sentence or is lengthy. Include the period as well in these cases. Do not capitalize the first word and use commas (or semicolons as described above) if the bullet items consist of one or a few words and merely complete the sentence introducing them. For example:

  Laboratory quality control (QC) samples will include:
  - method blanks,
  - laboratory control sample duplicates, and
  - matrix spike duplicate samples.

4.9   Measurements

- Use figures (i.e., don't spell out) for numbers that refer to measurements: 8 cm wide, 9 percent, 8 years old, 5-mg dose, 4 miles, 6 minutes, 3 inches, 7 acres.

- Spell out simple units in the text, such as inch, acre, liter, minute, and year. But if they are part of a complex unit, use the abbreviation (define first use just as you would with any abbreviation): ft/min, mg/L.

- Abbreviated measurements are written the same whether singular or plural. For example, lb can refer to both pound and pounds.

- Most measurement abbreviations do not take a period. Some do, however (in. for inch). See the list of measurement abbreviations in Section 13.0 to be sure.

4.10   Numbers

- Generally, spell out numbers less than 10 (one, three), and use numerals for 10 and higher (14, 256).

- Always use numerals to express measurement (2 feet, 4 mg/L, 7 gmp, 5 pore volumes), time (10 p.m.), parts of a document (Chapter 4, Phase 4, Section 2, Item 3, Table 6-1, Figure 2-3), money ($3 million), very large numbers followed by million or billion (7 million), percentages and decimal fractions (3 percent, 3.14, 1.2), and ratios (1 to 10).

- When two or more numbers are listed in a group in the same sentence, and one or more is 10 or more, use numerals for all:

  — The laboratory evaluated 7 of the 12 samples.

  — The contractor drilled 12 borings to a depth of 70 feet and completed 4 of the 12 borings as vapor extraction wells.

  — The contractor drilled six borings to a depth of 70 feet and completed four of the six borings as vapor extraction wells.

- Spell out all numbers that start a sentence: Twelve test holes were analyzed. You can also rewrite the sentence to move the number: *XYZ Company* analyzed 12 test holes.

- When numbers appear together in the same phrase, it is often a good practice to express one as a word and one as a number (XYZ *Company* purchased fourteen 8-inch pipes) but not in a list (XYZ *Company* purchased 6-, 8-, and 12-inch pipes).

- Use a comma in numbers larger than 999: 12,000, 9,000, 800.

- Use Arabic (1, 2, 3), not Roman (I, II, III), numerals for figures, illustrations, and tables.

- Change Roman numerals to Arabic in references, even when Roman numerals are used in the work itself: (Example: USEPA Region 10, Phase 3).

4.11   Parallelism

This is an important—albeit confusing—topic for technical writers, especially since we use so many lists. Basically, the elements in a list must all have the same grammatical structure. They must each flow individually from the introductory sentence. Make sure all the elements in a bulleted list, for example, are parallel to each other. If you begin one item with a verb, for example, all items must begin with a verb. The beginning of a list is the most important part; if necessary, it is acceptable to add additional elements to one or more items (see final example, below).

Incorrect: I like to do the following: flying an airplane, ride a bicycle, and shooting a gun.

Correct: I like to do the following: flying an airplane, riding a bicycle, and shooting a gun.

Incorrect: My dog is old, ugly, and he has a disease.

Correct: My dog is old, ugly, and diseased.

Incorrect: Approximately half the landfill was open to the public, and 25 percent was under development.

Correct: Approximately 50 percent of the landfill was open to the public, and 25 percent was under development.

Incorrect:
- Drill borings

- Installing wells
- Collection of samples

Correct:
- Drill borings
- Install wells
- Collect samples

Incorrect:

The objectives of this investigation were as follows:

- To determine the extent of petroleum-hydrocarbon impacted soils in the areas of confirmed impact.

- Determining the potential presence of petroleum-hydrocarbon impact to soil and water along the eastern edge of the pad.

- Collect subsurface hydrogeologic information.

- Collect such data as may be necessary, including identifying physical characteristics of the site, to support development of corrective actions and RBCLs, if warranted.

Correct:

The objectives of this investigation were as follows:

- To determine the extent of petroleum-hydrocarbon impacted soils in the areas of confirmed impact.

- To determine the potential presence of petroleum-hydrocarbon impact to soil and water along the eastern edge of the pad.

- To collect subsurface hydrogeologic information.

- To collect such data as may be necessary, including identifying physical characteristics of the site, to support development of corrective actions and RBCLs, if warranted.

4.12 References in the Text

- All that is necessary in the text is the author's last name and the year of publication (Smith, 1989). The complete information is found in the reference section. However, if you choose to give the author's full name first use or to list the title, that is acceptable.

- Use a semicolon to separate two or more references in the text (XYZ Company, 1993; USEPA, 1999).

- If the same author has more than one publication from the same year listed in the references section, use "a," "b," etc. (XYZ Company, 1999a).

- Note that commas follow the last name in our company's style (Jones, 2000).

4.13 Spacing

- Our company's style is to put one space after a period.

- There should only be one space after a comma, semicolon, or colon.

- The spacing of ellipsis points is (space) dot (space) dot (space) dot (space). Example: Mr. Rogers said that "easy children are . . . wonderful."

- The spacing of ellipsis points with an end period is (no space) dot (space) dot (space) dot (space). Example: According to NOAA, "The data are incomplete. . . ."

4.14 Spelling

- Use *Merriam-Webster's New Collegiate Dictionary* (m-w.com) as a standard spelling reference. If there is a choice of two spellings, use the first one (for example, canceled rather than cancelled).

- A list of commonly misspelled words is included in the Section 10.0 of this style guide.

- Watch for the following plurals, and remember that plural nouns take plural verbs. Singular: datum, matrix, phenomenon, schema. Plural: data, matrices, phenomena, schemas. The data are, the datum is . . .

4.14.1 Change British Spelling to American English

If you are asked to edit a British document for an American company, or vice versa, this list (Table 4-1) of the main differences between British and American spelling should make your task easier.

Table 4-1   British and American Spelling Differences

British	American
-our (vapour, colour)	-or (vapor, color)
-re (centre, metre)	-er (center, meter)
-ogue (dialogue)	-og (dialog)
-ence (defence)	-ense (defense)
-ise (minimise)	-ize (minimize)
-ising (utilising)	-izing (utilizing)
-isation (utilization)	-ization (utilization)
-isance (cognisance)	-izance (cognizance)
manoeuvred	maneuvered
learnt	learned
traveller	traveler
modelled	modeled
aluminium	aluminum
sulphide	sulfide
whilst	while
programme	program
judgement	judgment
towards	toward

American English spelling sometimes does not double the consonant at the end of a word, while British English spelling does, especially when the consonant is an "L"; for example, *travel, traveller, travelling* (U.K.) and *travel, traveler, traveling* (U.S.).

Also, note that U.S. English differs for the following (these are U.S.): single quotes inside double quotes, brackets inside parentheses.

4.15   Temperatures

- Use the numeral, the degree symbol, and either "F" or "C" for temperatures. Example: The temperature was 14 °F inside the building.

- Be consistent with using either F or C. U.S. companies will often give the temperature in Fahrenheit first, then in Celsius in parentheses, as in the following example:

  - The water temperature shall not be less than 40 °F (4.4 °C).

- The correct definitions and spellings are Fahrenheit (F) and Celsius (C). Some companies use "Centigrade" instead of "Celsius," but our company's style is to use Celsius.

4.16   Tense

In general, technical writers use present tense unless referring to past events. In those cases, use past tense. Proposals will probably also use future tense (*XYZ Company will evaluate the data*). Refer to other sources in past tense (*Smith said that . . .*). Discuss past results of tests in past tense (*One water sample was analyzed for VOCs*). Discuss final results and conclusions in present tense (*the results indicate*). Following are examples of correct tense usage:

- John Smith said, "I don't think so."

- The landfill was evaluated by Jane Doe, who said at the time, "There are clear violations here."

- Janet Smith, in *The Making of a Great Disposal Area*, wrote, "Efficiency is the most important thing."

- If the participant is finished answering the questions, the data are complete.

- Since that time, investigators from several studies have used this method.

- The CERCLA investigation includes the following. . . .

- Successfully completing site investigation or RI/FS projects has been the subcontractor's main focus since 1990.

- The group was formed to provide a core of specialists to the FAA. . . .

- The company's field staff members are trained to . . .

- Examples of site investigations XYZ Company has performed in Alaska include. . . .

- This report includes seven sections and two appendices.

- Section 1.0 contains the report introduction. . . .

- XYZ Company is recognized as a leading groundwater consulting firm.

4.17   Time

- Use a.m. and p.m. (note lowercase and periods) when included with the time: 10 a.m.

- Do not define a.m. and p.m.

- Use numerals when referring to a specific time, even if the number is less than 10. Example: The company ran the test at 3 p.m. and again at 9 p.m.

- Do not put two periods next to each other, even if a.m. or p.m. end the sentence. Example: The company ran a final test at 1 a.m.

- Do not put o'clock or :00 after the time if it is on the hour (Example: Sample collection occurred between 11 a.m. and 1 p.m.). But do use a colon and a numeral when giving specific times that are not on the hour (Examples: 2:15 p.m., 4:32 a.m.).

- If you are referring to a nonspecific time, do not use a.m. or p.m. Example: The company representatives arrived in the afternoon. But generally, in technical writing, we try to be exact, so use the correct time if you can.

4.18   Titles and Names of People

- Capitalize titles only when they directly precede a person's name or are part of an address: The source of the information was Project Manager Jane Szmanski. The project manager is Jane Szmanski. Jane Szmanski, project manager, is . . .

- Do not use a hyphen in vice president.

- In the text, give the person's full name the first mention. From then on, use Mr. or Ms. before the last name. If you are not sure of the person's gender, continue using the full name. Examples: John Smith, Mr. Smith; Sally Jones, Ms. Jones; Pat Johnson, Pat Johnson.

4.19   Unbiased Language

By now we all know we should write language that is inoffensive, but sometimes it is difficult to know what to replace words with. Sometimes the correction may seem wordy or awkward. Often the simplest way to avoid using *he/she* or *he and she* is to make the subject plural. For example, replace "An English teacher has little time to read anything except his or her students' papers" with "English teachers have little time to read anything except student papers." Modern English handbooks contain many suggestions for revising to eliminate biased language. Table 4-1 contains examples from the *Publication Manual of the American Psychological Association.*

Table 4-2   Replacing Biased Language with Unbiased Language

Replace:	With:
The client is the best judge of his counseling.	Clients are the best judges of the counseling they receive. The client is the best judge of the value of counseling.
man, mankind	people, humanity, human beings, humankind, humans
man a project	staff a project, hire personnel, employ staff
manpower	workforce, personnel, workers, human resources
woman doctor, lady lawyer, male nurse, woman driver	physician, lawyer, nurse, driver
chairman	chair, chairperson
foreman	supervisor or superintendent
Eskimos	Inuit, Aleuts (be specific)
disabled person, mentally ill person	person with a disability, person with mental illness
stroke victim, suffering from multiple sclerosis, confined to a wheelchair	individual who had a stroke, people who have multiple sclerosis, uses a wheelchair

Source: *Publication Manual of the American Psychological Association*

5.0 WRITING TIPS

The purpose of this section is to help you make your writing sharp and clear and to point out common errors to avoid, such as using clichés.

5.1 Overview

No matter what type of writing you are doing, technical or not, consider two things as most important: (1) audience, and (2) ethos (or your writer's tone; how you come across). Try to consider your audience when you write, and do not expect your readers to be experts in your subject matter or to know the definitions of the terms, acronyms, and abbreviations you are using. At the same time, consider your "ethos" by not writing "down" to your audience. You want to approach your subject matter with both respect for the readers and clarity.

Often, as a technical editor, my job is to tell the author, "This doesn't make sense to me here. Can you clarify?" I represent the "nonexpert" audience, and I try to read from this perspective, so I can tell the writer exactly where the writing might "lose" the readers.

You, as the writer, and an expert on the subject, might know what you mean, but did you really explain it to the reader in a clear, concise manner? Other questions to consider include:

- Are all tables and figures explained fully in the text before they appear?

- Do the tables make sense on their own?

- Can the reader follow your organization?

Outlines can be handy tools to use before actually writing, as discussed in Section 4.5. Personally, I prefer to make an outline before I am going to write technical material. Your outline can be just a few notes, a list of major (and perhaps minor) headings, or a full-on list of every paragraph in the document. Whatever helps you organize the material best is the method to use.

It may be necessary to go back after writing and reorganize sections. Some writers work better getting the material down quickly, and then going back and reshaping it.

If you are "stuck," or feel that your document is not flowing well, do not hesitate to ask the technical editor for help.

5.2   Getting Started

Here are some tips that may help you get started in writing your document. An English handbook also provides many ideas for beginning the writing process, outlining your ideas, and organizing your material. Therefore, if you have "writer's block," it might also be useful to look through those sections in a handbook. Here are steps to take before you begin writing:

1. Gather information and data (think about what you want to say).

2. Identify and refine your document's purpose (consider why you are going to say it).

3. Identify your audience (determine who you are going to say it to).

4. Organize your information and ideas (decide how you are going to say it).

For Step 4, it is useful to make an outline. Your outline can be changed, of course, but it will often lead you to knowing your headings and subheadings and where to put specific material in your document. A writer might find it easier to write the outline as a Table of Contents page.

The next step is actually writing the draft. You can write sections out of order, if needed. Do not worry about grammar, punctuation, and style at this point. Just get something down.

After you have your draft written, go ahead and do your revisions. If you have time to set it aside a day, go ahead and do so. As you revise, aim to clarify, strengthen, and condense your message. Also, check the overall organization. This is also the time to go back and write the introductory material, such as the Transmittal Letter and Executive Summary, if needed in this report.

As you revise, here are some questions that might assist you:

- Does the reader know what the report, section, or paragraph is about? If not, make sure you have the topic sentences or main ideas listed first. Example: "This section evaluates the data collected from the three well sites."

- What does the audience most likely want to know? Check any materials you have (bid packet, report guidelines, previous reports, original proposal) to make sure you have provided the necessary information.

- How well organized is the document?

- Are there any gaps in logic or information?

- Is there enough supporting material (i.e., figures, tables, graphs)?

- Did you use transitional words and phrases (therefore, furthermore, for example, however, in fact, also, first, second, finally, consequently, in addition, on the other hand, next, in conclusion, as a result, in the same way, in other words, in contrast, most important, further, to summarize)?

- How well did you say it? Do you have awkward sentences? Have you checked for the following problem areas (this is also done by the technical editor): sentence structure, sentence variety, subject-verb agreement, passive voice, wordiness, misuse of pronouns, misplaced modifiers, faulty parallelism, poor organization, and poor formatting? Use your handbook or this style guide for suggestions on improving these areas.

- Did you leave anything out that is essential to fulfilling the requirements of the document?

- Did you include information that is not relevant?

- Did you use specific, concrete language? Can a nonexpert read your document?

- Did you avoid jargon, clichés, and wordiness?

- Did you use enough headings and bullet lists to add to readability?

5.3   Active and Passive Voice

"Don't use passive voice," is probably one of those red-ink English teacher comments you sometimes saw but that was never explained. Active voice is preferred because it is easier to read and to understand, so it is especially important in technical material. Basically, in the active voice, the subject comes first. Another way to look at it is that the subject does the acting.

ACTIVE: The contractor evaluated the data.

In passive voice, the subject is acted upon. The reason this is a problem is that it is wordy and harder to follow.

PASSIVE: The data were evaluated by the contractor.

5.4   Be Specific

Technical writers should be as clear and specific as possible, avoiding vague language. Therefore, if you are seeing words like "many, some, a few" in a document, it probably needs revising. Instead of writing "a very high concentration," for example, give the exact measurement. Give the depth of a test pit rather than just calling it "shallow" or "deep." Instead of merely saying something is "contaminated," provide the reader with the amount by which the standard is exceeded and specifically name the compounds involved. Instead of saying something is satisfactory, state exactly which standards or regulations it meets.

5.5   Clichés

Avoid clichés like the plague; they are overused expressions that have lost their meaning. Even if you are blind as a bat, you can see a cliché for what it is: nothing.

5.6   Jargon

One of the main goals of technical writers is to make text clear and simple. One of the ways this is done is by replacing jargon with simple, clear language. Jargon is technical vocabulary, and it is often not necessary. One of the best things to happen to technical writing in the last 20 years is the elimination of jargon and the increase in readability of documents. Writing jargon or extra words (such as this example from APA: "monetarily felt scarcity" instead of "poverty") prevents readers from understanding the text. Here is an example from another company's style guide:

> Winston Churchill, facing Hitler's armed forces in 1940, said to Americans, "Give us the tools, and we will do the job." He did not say, "Supply us with the necessary

inputs of relevant equipment, and we will implement the
program and accomplish its objectives."

Table 5-1 contains examples of jargon and ways to correct them.

Table 5-1   Simplifying Jargon

Replace	With
adjacent to	next to, beside, near, adjoining
atop	on
currently	now
per your request	as requested
observed	saw
presently	now
prior to	before
with regard to, relating to	about, for, of
reside	live
residential structure	residence
stated	said
subsequent to	after
upon	on
usage	use
utilize	use
with respect to	about

Source: *Chicago Manual of Style*

5.7   Sentence Errors

Comma splices, fragments, and run-on sentences are the three most
common sentence errors. Any English handbook contains detailed
definitions of each of these, but here are examples for your reference.

Comma Splice: A comma splice has a complete sentence before the
comma, it also has a complete sentence after the comma.

How to correct: Use a period or a semicolon instead of a comma, or add
a coordinating conjunction after the comma (and, but, or, for, so, yet).

Fragment: An incomplete thought. Fragments are unfinished because. All
sentences need, at a minimum. A subject and a verb.

How to correct: If it sounds incomplete, it is probably a fragment. Revise the sentence.

Run-ons: Run-on sentences are two sentences crashed together they have no punctuation in between them.

How to correct: The easiest way to correct run-on sentences is to put a period or semicolon in between the two sentences.

5.8   Vague Terms

Try to avoid using "it" and vague pronoun references. State exactly who or what you mean.

CONFUSING: Columbia Analytical Services gave the results to XYZ Company. It then gave the results to the client's representatives. They . . .

CLARIFIED: Columbia Analytical Services gave the results to XYZ Company. XYZ Company gave a copy of the results to the client, Company A. Company A then . . .

Also, note that a company is singular, so you would not use "they" when referring to a company. This is where you will sometimes use "it," but make sure your text is clear on who or what "it" refers to.

5.9   Wordiness

Technical writing should be "tight" and clear. If you can use one word instead of three or four, do so. The main problem with wordiness is that it makes the text hard to read. Table 5-2 shows some shorter alternatives to wordy phrases such as using "for" instead of "for the purposes of."

Another way to eliminate wordiness is to avoid redundant phrases. In the following examples from APA, the italicized words are redundant and should be eliminated: *one and* the same, in *close* proximity, *completely* unanimous, *period of* time, summarize *briefly*, the reason is *because*, has been *previously* found, small *in size*, *a total of* 68 participants, *both* alike, four *different* groups.

Table 5-2   Eliminating Wordiness

Wordy Phrase	Better
a 7-year period	7 years
a large number of	many

Wordy Phrase	Better
ahead of schedule	early
as to whether	whether
at this point in time	now
based on the fact that	because
blue in color	blue
close proximity	proximity
conduct interviews with	interview
consensus of opinion	consensus
constructed in two levels	two-story
contained within	in
designated, termed, named as	designated, termed, named
developed for residential use	residential
divided into four quarters	divided into quarters
during the time that	while, when
end product	product
few in number	few
fine-grained in texture	fine-grained
first priority	priority
for the purpose of assessing	to assess
for the purpose of	for, to
future potential	potential
immediately adjacent to	next to, beside, adjoining
in a shingle-type method	like shingles
in advance of	before
in excess of	over, exceeding
in order to accomplish	to accomplish
in proximity to	near
in regard to, in relation to	regarding, about, of
in the event that	if
in the near future	soon
in the vicinity of	near, about
infiltrate through	infiltrate
integral part	part
is in a muddy condition	is muddy
is to be established	will be established

Wordy Phrase	Better
it is *Company*'s understanding	*Company* understands
may, might possibly	may, might
of a similar nature, similar in nature	similar
on a monthly (weekly) basis	monthly (weekly)
on an as-needed basis	as needed
performed a site reconnaissance	reconnoitered (the site)
prior to the collection of samples	before samples are collected
results so far achieved	results so far
the present study	this study
there were several students who completed	12 students completed
to the point that	enough, sufficiently
topographic features	topography
were used for the storage of	stored
work, tasks performed	work, tasks

Source: *Chicago Manual of Style*

5.10   Words to Avoid for Liability Reasons

Try to avoid overstating or overpromising. Be careful with word selection. Make sure if you use the following words and ones similar to them that you are not promising or saying too much: all, none, always, never, any, eliminate, stop, equal, guarantee, warrant, certify, ensure, insure, best, highest, maximum, minimum.

There are other words available in this rich English language that should serve your purposes just as well, depending on the context, such as sufficient, typical, facilitate, monitor, equivalent, similar, limit, reduce, recommend, and review.

Here is an example: Instead of *XYZ Company guarantees to provide the client with the best choice*, write *XYZ Company will advise the client on the most appropriate action.*

6.0   STANDARD DOCUMENT FORMATTING

Overall, most companies prefer block format for all technical documents. Block format means that paragraphs are single spaced (or perhaps 1.15 as shown on Figure 6-1, below), with a full paragraph space above (also shown on Figure 6-1; in this case, I inserted 12 points above each paragraph and 0 points below; this would be standard when the font size for "normal" text in the document is also 12 points). Headings should also have 12 points above and 0 points below.

Most companies seem to prefer left justification for reports and other documents as well. This is easier to read. However, full justification can look more professional, so this is your decision.

There should only be one space after a period, colon, or semicolon. This changed since the "typewriter days," when two spaces were called for after a period. Now it is easy to search and replace two spaces with one throughout an entire document.

I have formatted the book form of this document to model what I suggest:

- Times New Roman 11-point font for normal text.

- Arial bold font for headings

- One space after periods, commas, and semicolons.

- Block format (11 points above each single-spaced paragraph).

- Figure and table captions before the figure and table, and always referenced in the text before they appear. (Note that some disagree with me on this and still put the figure captions below, or after, the figure. As an editor, I accept and use the company's style I am working with. But I prefer to have the caption before the figure so that I can add notes below the figure and so that a short title can be used that will be included in the automated Table of Contents.)

Figure 6-1   Paragraph Spacing for Technical Documents

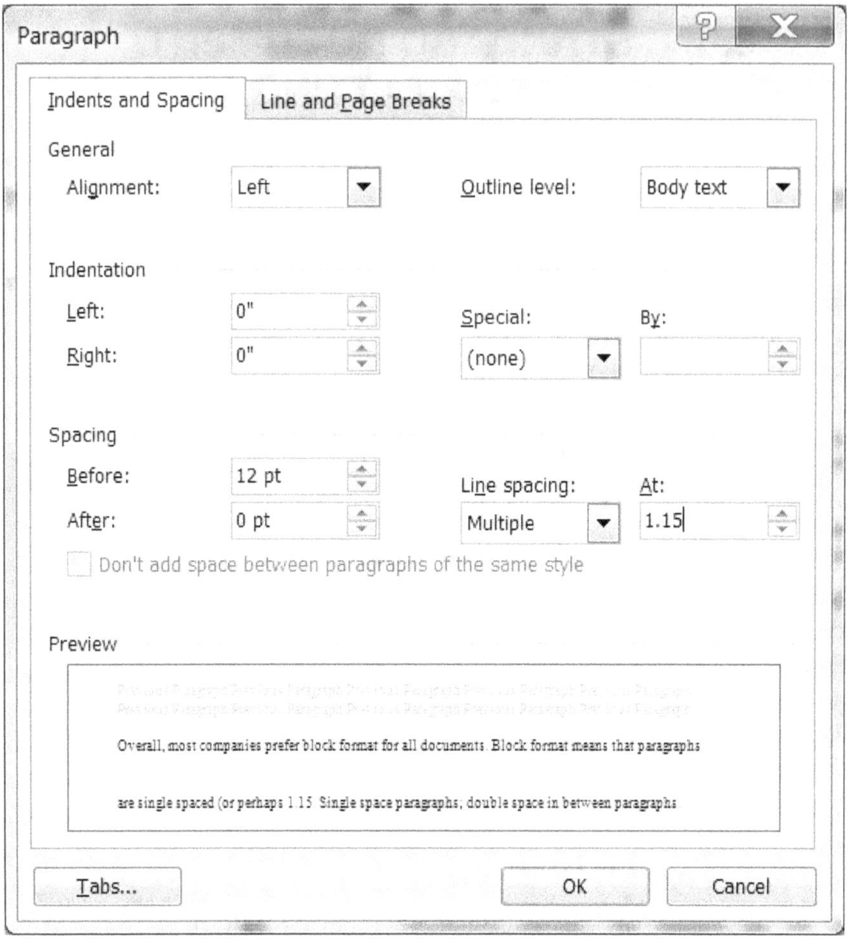

6.1   Memorandum

The standard format for memoranda is as follows:

Margins: 1 inch from top, bottom, and both sides.

Justification: Memos are fully justified.

Font: Text font is Times New Roman 11 points.

Use your company's stationery.

Introductory material: The template has the necessary information in the following order:

Date:

To:

From:

Subject:

Signature: Memos are not signed.

Spacing: single-spaced paragraphs with a double space between each paragraph.

End: At the end of a memo, always include the following:

Attachments

Enclosures (if any)

cc: file (and any other names or places copies are going)

Length: A memo should only be one or two pages; if more than one page, consider using a letter format instead.

6.2   Transmittal Letter

A transmittal letter is sometimes included in the front matter of a lengthy (40 or more pages) report. Here are some features of the transmittal letter:

- A letter is usually one page. Short one-page letters usually have three paragraphs: introduction, body, and closing.

- The language is not technical.

- The letter documents when the report was sent, how it was sent, to whom it was addressed, how many copies were sent, and who was responsible for preparing the report.

- A letter does not use acronyms and abbreviations.

- The letter is addressed to a specific person (Dear Mr. Jones:).

- Distribution is noted on the bottom left (cc.).

- The letter also clarifies if it is a draft report, and, if so, when comments are due back and how.

- The letter indicates, if it is a draft, what is missing from the report (if anything) and when the missing information will be available.

- The letter closes by thanking the client and using the word "Sincerely,".

6.3   Standard Report

6.3.1   Document Organization

The standard document contains the following elements in this order:

- Title page

- Any preface materials (such as a transmittal letter)

- Table of Contents

- List of Appendices

- List of Figures and Tables

- List of Acronyms and Abbreviations

- Section 1.0 Executive Summary

- Section 2.0 Introduction

- Other sections, leading up to the Conclusions and Recommendations Section

- References

- Appendices

6.3.2   Spacing and Text Fonts

- Use single space text.

- Use Times New Roman 11 point font.

- If we use 11-point font, set "normal" style for 11 points before each paragraph for block paragraphing. If we use 12-point font, set normal for 12 points above (or before) each paragraph.

- Use only one space after a period, semicolon, or colon.

- Text should be left justification; shorter company documents may be fully justified.

6.3.3 Section Headings

Each section contains up to five levels of headings, which are formatted as follows:

- Caps, centered, bold, Arial 14, NUMBER AT LEFT IS 4.0

- All caps, left justified, bold, Arial 12, NUMBER AT LEFT IS 4.1

- Upper and lowercase, left, bold, Arial 11, NUMBER AT LEFT IS 4.1.1

- Upper and lowercase, number is indented .5 (1 tab), no bold, italic, Arial 10, NUMBER AT LEFT IS 4.1.1.1

- Fifth-level heading. Italics, Arial 10, underlined, DON'T USE NUMBER AT LEFT

The Table of Contents should be formatted so that only headings 1 through 3 are shown there.

Title Page

The title page should include the following:

- Report title

- Type of report (interim, internal, progress, draft, final)

- Contract, delivery, and job order numbers

- Date

- Client (Prepared for) name and address

- Client logo if available

- Company Name (Prepared by) name and address

- Terra logo

Table of Contents Page

- The header, **TABLE OF CONTENTS**, should be centered and bold.

- Items in the Table of Contents (TOC) should be all caps or initial caps, just as they appear in the text headings.

- No bold or underscores are used in the TOC.

- Second and third-level headings are indented.

- TOCs use up to third-level headings.

- Multivolume reports should each have their own individual TOCs.

List of Tables and Figures

- Use the heading "**LIST OF TABLES AND FIGURES**" all bold and caps at top of the page.

- Begin the List of Tables and Figures on a separate page from the TOC.

- Numbering is handled with hyphens: Figure 1-1.

- Items are in upper/lowercase (title case), no bold.

- If you use the caption command correctly in the text, you should never have to type in the titles and page numbers; just insert the Table of Contents, Tables, and then the Table of Contents, Figures.

List of Appendices

- The List of Appendices (if needed) is placed after the List of Tables and Figures. If it fits, it can be on the same page as the List of Tables and Figures (see example, next page).

- Use the following format for the Appendices TOC:

  LIST OF APPENDICES

  Appendix A   Title Here

  Appendix B   Title Here

- Note that no page numbers are listed for the List of Appendices since they do not actually have page numbers. If they are lengthy documents of themselves that do include page numbers, number each page as A-1, A-2, etc. for Appendix A, and B-1, B-2, etc. for Appendix B.

List of Acronyms and Abbreviations

- Our company places the acronyms list at the front of the document, between the TOC and the Executive Summary. (Some documents are different; for example, Site Technical Practices [CRTs and STPs] include the Abbreviations and Acronyms as Section 4.)

- All acronyms used in the report, including in figures, tables, and appendices, must be included.

- Use the acronyms and abbreviations list in Section 13.0 of this style guide for guidance on capitalization and spelling.

- Be sure the entries are in alphabetical order.

Executive Summary

- Reports more than 40 pages should have an Executive Summary. It is helpful to the reader to have an Executive Summary even if the report is shorter than 40 pages.

- The Executive Summary states the purpose and nature of the investigation; provides a brief account of the approach used; and includes the major results, conclusions, and recommendations.

- The Executive Summary has its own page numbers in the format "ES-#," as in ES-1, ES-2, etc. This emphasizes that the Executive Summary can stand alone.

- Acronyms are defined in the Executive Summary as if it is a separate document that will stand on its own. Do not use them heavily.

- Though unusual in an Executive Summary, if you include Tables or Figures, number them as follows: Figure ES-1.

Report Pages

- Each main section begins on a right-hand page.

- Page numbering is based on the section. For example, page 3-2 means Section 3, page 2.

- Documents are normally printed on both sides of the page if the report is longer than 50 pages.

- Blank pages may be necessary when there is an 11x17 (foldout) figure or table because the foldout must begin on an odd-numbered page. The page after the foldout is also blank. Both blank pages are still counted in page numbering, however.

- Text font is 12 pt. Times, no bold.

- Standard practice for reports is full justification.

- Reports are usually printed on 8.5- x 11-inch white paper, single column.

- Report headings are usually 1.0, 1.1., 1.1.1, 1.1.1.1. Most companies prefer no number on heading levels 5, 6, etc. The figures below show the general and the outline number settings for Headings 1 and 2 in Microsoft Word (your preferred font type and size might be different than Arial 16 bold as I have for Heading 1, shown on Figure 6-2).

Figure 6-2   Heading 1 General Guidelines

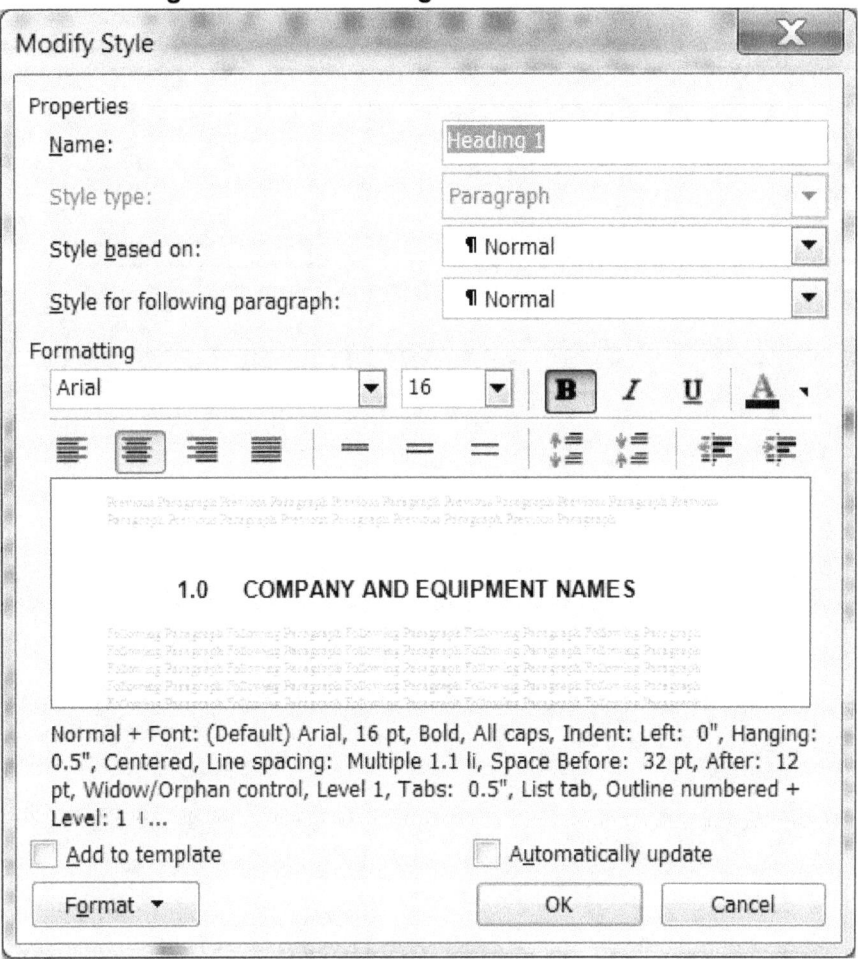

Figure 6-3 Heading 1 Outline Number Settings in Word

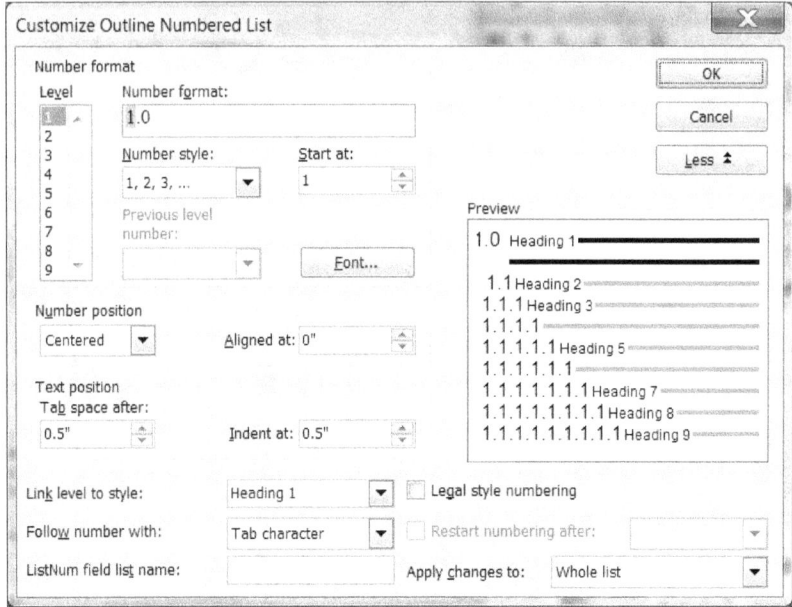

Figure 6-4 Heading 2 Outline Number Settings in Word

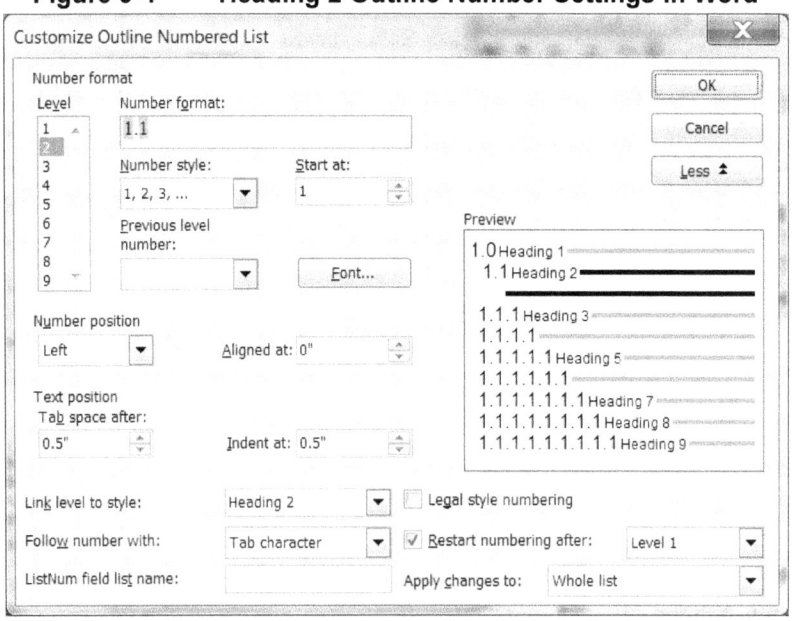

If you do not have a report template already, Wordsworth LLC (www.wordsworthwriting.net) sells report and proposal templates, as well as numerous other templates, with the heading and other styles already created and instructions inserted. The same documents, as well as thousands of government and business forms, can be purchased at Forms in Word (www.formsinword.com).

Figures and Tables

- Tables and figures are numbered according to the overall sections they are in. The second number has nothing to do with the subsections (second-, third-, and fourth-level headings); it is based on the table's order in that section. Therefore, Table 3-3 is the third table in Section 3 of the report.

- Capitalize the words *table* and *figure* only when they are used with a specific number (Table 4-4, the table).

- Use a hyphen, not a period, to separate table numbers (Table 5-7).

- Tables and figures appear after the first mention, either on the same page after the text mention or on the following page. They must be referred to in the text. Example: Figure 4-2, Site Location, identifies four areas of concern.

- Figure and table fonts are as follows: Arial 10, bold, centered. Then insert a tab before typing the title in title case (the reason for the tab instead of spaces is that it looks nicer in the Table of Contents). Table 6-1 and Figure 6-5 are examples.

Table 6-1   Cook Inlet Survey Data – 2002

Title Here – Bold and Centered	Title Here – 10 pt.	Title Here
Text in this column is usually left justified	Text in all other columns is usually centered	Text – All text is 10 pts.
Text	Text	Text
Text	Text	Text

Title Here – Bold and Centered	Title Here – 10 pt.	Title Here

Notes:

1. Always include definitions to all acronyms and notes below in smaller, indented font. Here I used 8 pt. font, Arial, no bold, left justified.
2. Note that the cells are merged here, and only the top border shows. Or you can include the notes below the table, and not within a cell.
3. Always "repeat" the header row, in case the table goes to a second page.

Key:

ADEC   Alaska Department of Environmental Conservation

USEPA   U.S. Environmental Protection Agency

Figure 6-5   Crevasse Moraine Trails

Notes:

1. I prefer to put figure captions above the figure, the same as table captions, so that I can have room for notes below a figure. I also prefer the look of the short figure captions that look nice in the Table of Contents.
2. Some companies prefer to add a third caption type, Photo, instead of using the word "Figure" for photographs.
3. I create a style called Table Notes that is smaller than the text and caption font and is set .2 spaces in, so that it is indented beneath the table. It has 2 points space before and 0 after. I use this same style for the blank paragraph under each figure and table (or after the last note if there are notes).

References

The format of references is a stylistic matter. There is no right or wrong (unless you are writing for a certain agency or company that has its own style guide). It may seem that there are almost as many reference styles as there are books. The main point is to be consistent—both throughout a document and throughout a company.

I prefer to base my references on *Chicago Manual of Style*, with some slight changes based on the hundreds of companies I have edited for. However, there are excellent online sources on Chicago Manual of style (such as this one for government citations at http://library.bowdoin.edu/help/chicago-gov.pdf or this one on general citations at http://www.chicagomanualofstyle.org/tools_citationguide.html), so Chicago might be a good one to follow). Within a month's time, I might use 10 different references styles, depending on what the client's needs are. Government agencies often have their own style guidelines; specific companies have their own style guides; academic writing has its own preferences [MLA, APA, etc.); newspapers and magazines might use AP or Chicago or their own guides). I believe the references sections is the most difficult part of a report because to find out what that particular company's preferences are and then to make all the entries (which can sometimes be in the hundreds) consistent are tricky. I also need (if the client understands the time involved in doing this correctly) to check every link to make sure it works and the spelling of titles and authors, as well as the dates, to be sure they are accurate.

My in-text citations usually just include the author (or agency) and the year. Whether or not to use a comma in between is again your choice, but be consistent; if the company has no preference, I leave out the commas, as in these examples: (Abrams 2012) (USFS 2014) (Coletta and Nagy 2014).

General Guidelines for References Section

Below are some overall guidelines to follow if your company does not have its own references style. The main point to keep in mind is to be consistent throughout your document. The main thing is to remember to be consistent. Your readers need to be able to find your references, if needed, so give them enough information to do so.

Entries should be alphabetically arranged by author's last name (first author listed in original text). If there is no author, list under the title. The order and description within entries are as follows:

1. Author(s) or editor(s). Spell out the names of authors and editors in the text as they appear on the title page of the document. Avoid using "et al." (which stands for "and others") in this list unless there are more than six authors' names; reserve et al. for the text when there are more than three authors.

2. Date. List the year of publication or "n.d." if there is no date available. If there are two or more reports by the same author in the same year, add a, b, c, etc. to the date in both text and list.

3. Title. Titles are typed in capital and lowercase letters (title case). Titles are either italicized, placed within quotation marks, or typed with no italics or quotation marks according to the following rules:

    —   Books and reports. Italicize titles of all separate, freestanding, printed publications. Use standard capitalization rules, and spell out titles completely.

    —   Journal articles, papers in proceedings, and manuscripts in collections. Titles of material contained within larger documents are put in quotation marks; the name of the larger work is italicized and spelled out in full.

    —   Regulations and statutes. Titles of regulations and statutes are typed with no underline or quotation marks.

4. Editor, if entry by author.

5. Symposium or proceedings dates and locations in parentheses, if not part of the title.

6. Volume number.

7. Government or agency report number.

8. Mention of draft status, if applicable.

9. Revision or edition number.

10. Publisher.

11. Location of publisher (if a book). Use the two-letter U.S. Postal Service codes for state names. Publisher and location are not required when referencing a periodical (journal or magazine).

12. Page numbers (if an article). Insert the inclusive page numbers for articles within journals, proceedings, and technical reports,

preceded by "pp." if more than one page, or by "p." if only one page.

13. Month (and day, if available), if needed to distinguish between drafts, etc.

14. Web site accessed month, day, year: full link (if applicable).

6.3.4 Sample References Section

Note: These examples are in the style I use when a company has no preference; they aren't exactly *Chicago Manual of Style*, but close to it, and based on the list in Section 6.12.1 of this document.

Alaska Administrative Code. 2003. 5 AAC § 75.222 Policy for the Management of Sustainable Wild Trout Fisheries. Juneau, Alaska.

Alaska Department of Environmental Conservation (ADEC). 2012. *Alaska DEC User's Manual. Best Management Practices for Gravel/Rock Aggregate Extraction Projects: Protecting Surface Water and Groundwater Quality in Alaska.* Prepared by Shannon & Wilson, Inc. September. Web site accessed December 17, 2014: http://dec.alaska.gov/water/wnpspc/protection_restoration/bestm gmtpractices/Docs/GravelRockExtractionBMPManual.pdf.

Alaska Department of Fish and Game (ADF&G). 2014. Subsistence Regulations. Web site accessed August 14, 2013: http://www.adfg.alaska.gov/index.cfm?adfg=subsistenceregulati ons.main.

Alaska Energy Authority (AEA). 2012a. Renewable Energy Fund Round 6. Web site: http://www.akenergyauthority.org/RE_Fund-6.html. July.

Alaska Energy Authority (AEA). 2012b. Power Cost Equalization. Web site: http://www.akenergyauthority.org/programspce.html

Alaska Energy Authority (AEA). 2010. Alaska Energy Plan Community Database. Web site: http://www.akenergyauthority.org/alaska-energy-plan.html

Gill, A.B., and M. Bartlett. 2010. *Literature Review on the Potential Effects of Electromagnetic Fields and Subsea Noise From*

Marine Renewable Energy Developments on Atlantic Salmon, Sea Trout and European Eel. Scottish Natural Heritage Commissioned Report No. 401.

Institute of Social and Economic Research (ISER), University of Alaska Anchorage. 2012a. Internal Publications Database Search. Web site: http://www.iser.uaa.alaska.edu/publications.php?id=1518.

Institute of Social and Economic Research (ISER), University of Alaska Anchorage. 2012b. *Alaska Fuel Price Projections 2012-2035.* ISER Working Paper 2012.1 and Microsoft Excel Spreadsheet Price Model. July.

National Fire Protection Association. 2008. National Electrical Code. (NFPA70). Quincy, MA: National Fire Protection Association.

National Marine Fisheries Service (NMFS). 2013. *2013 Steller Sea Lion Protection Measures for Groundfish Fisheries in the Bering Sea and Aleutian Islands Management Area.* Preliminary Draft EIS/RIR/IRFA. March. Web site accessed August 13, 2013: http://www.npfmc.org/protected-species/steller-sea-lions/.

Person, D.K., and A.L. Russell. 2009. "Reproduction and Den Site Selection by Wolves in a Disturbed Landscape." *Northwest Science.* 83(3): pp. 211-24.

Person, D.K., M. Kirchhoff, V. Van Ballenberghe, G.C. Iverson, and E. Grossman. 1996. *The Alexander Archipelago Wolf: A Conservation Assessment.* USDA General Technical Report PNW-GTR-384.

Piatt, J.F., N.L. Naslund, and T.I. Van Pelt. 1999. "Discovery of a New Kittlitz's Murrelet Nest: Clues to Habitat Selection and Nest-Site Fidelity." *Northwestern Naturalist.* 80: pp. 8-13.

U.S. Fish and Wildlife Service. 1985. *Habitat Suitability Models and Instream Flow Suitability Curves: Chum Salmon,* by S.S. Hale, T.E. McMahon, and P.C. Nelson. Biological Report 82 (10, 108). August.

6.4   Proposals

Proposals are a marketing tool, and therefore we can have a bit more flexibility as far as formatting goes. In general, use the same formatting as the report. That can be fine for a proposal as well. If it is agreed to by the writer, editor, and project manager, such formatting changes such as columns, headings with color, text boxes featuring quotes from clients and advantages to using our company, and changes in fonts may be used. No more than two or possibly three (say, for tables) fonts should be used within one document.

6.5 Resumes

There are four standard resumes used by our company. Brief descriptions of these follow. As soon as you begin working here, you should write your resumes (in all four formats) and give them to the technical editor for editing and formatting. Also, if you already work for our company, you should update your resume at least every 6 months and give your changes to the technical editor.

6.5.1 Resume: Standard Long Version

- Treat each resume as a separate document. This means it should stand on its own, so all acronyms should be defined first use.

- Long resumes can be two or more pages.

6.5.2 Resume: Short Version

- Treat each resume as a separate document. This means it should stand on its own, so all acronyms should be defined first use.

- The short version is usually one page; two pages can be used if necessary.

6.5.3 Resume: One Paragraph

- These are used in proposals as well as on our Web site.

- Remember to update them frequently and give your changes to the technical editor.

6.5.4 Resume: SF330 Form

- For certain government proposals, we are required to use what is called the SF330 form. The font size is usually 10 points.

- There are certain standard sections to each SF330 form. (This form is available in Microsoft Word from www.formsinword.com.) A sample resume page from Forms in Word's/Wordsworth's "Sample SF330 Form Filled Out" is shown as Figure 6-6.

Figure 6-6 Sample SF330 Resume Page

E. RESUMES OF KEY PERSONNEL PROPOSED FOR THIS CONTRACT
(Complete one Section E for each key person.)

12. NAME	13. ROLE IN THIS CONTRACT	14. YEARS EXPERIENCE: a. TOTAL	14. YEARS EXPERIENCE: b. WITH CURRENT FIRM
Darryl Rogain	Principal Architect & Quality Control	12	7

15. FIRM NAME AND LOCATION (City and State)
ROGAIN DESIGN GROUP PC

16. EDUCATION (DEGREE AND SPECIALIZATION)	17. CURRENT PROFESSIONAL REGISTRATION (STATE AND DISCIPLINE)
• Bachelor of Architecture, University of Alaska • Participant – ATFP Workshop, Naval Facilities Engineering Service Center, 1999	• Architecture – Alaska #1874; Maryland #1232-A • Alaska #1235; Georgia #12864 • NCARB Certificate #43996

18. OTHER PROFESSIONAL QUALIFICATIONS (Publications, Organizations, Training, Awards, etc.)

19. RELEVANT PROJECTS

	(1) TITLE AND LOCATION (City and State)	(2) YEAR COMPLETED: PROFESSIONAL SERVICES	(2) YEAR COMPLETED: CONSTRUCTION (If applicable)	(3) BRIEF DESCRIPTION (Brief scope, size, cost, etc.) AND SPECIFIC ROLE	Check if project performed with current firm
a.	Indefinite Quantity Contract for Architectural & Engineering Design Services for Various Projects, Army Base, Camp Lagoon, Alaska N62470-01-D-2002	2003	2004	Mr. Rogain was the principal architect and conducted quality control for numerous design/build projects at Camp Lagoon. Rogain Design Group provided design only on this project valued at $19.4 million. See Project #1 for complete details. Rogain's total cost was $1.2 million.	☒
b.	IDIQ Contract for Architectural & Engineering Design Services for Various Projects, Army Base, Camp Lagoon, Alaska N62470-00-D-4751	2002		Mr. Rogain was the principal architect and conducted quality control for numerous design/build projects at Camp Lagoon. Complete A&E services were provided for projects totaling $3.9 million under this IDIQ contract. See Project #2 for complete details.	☒
c.	IDIQ Contract for Architectural & Engineering Design Services for Various Projects, Army Base, Camp Lagoon, Alaska N62470-99-D-4087	2001		Mr. Rogain was the principal architect and conducted quality control for numerous design/build projects at Camp Lagoon. Complete A&E services were provided for projects totaling $7.56 million under this IDIQ contract. See Project #3 for complete details.	☒
d.	IDIQ Contract for Architectural & Engineering Design Services for Various Projects at Army Base, Camp Lagoon, Alaska N62470-98-D-3895	1999		Mr. Rogain was the principal architect and conducted quality control for numerous design/build projects at Camp Lagoon. Complete A&E services were provided for projects totaling $10.92 million under this IDIQ contract. See Project #4 for complete details.	☒
e.	IDIQ Contract for Architectural & Engineering Design Services for Various Projects, Army Base, Camp Lagoon, Alaska N62470-96-D-4486	1999		Mr. Rogain was the principal architect and conducted quality control for numerous design/build projects at Camp Lagoon. Complete A&E services were provided for projects totaling $6.074 million under this IDIQ contract. See Project #5 for complete details.	☐

7.0 USING THE REVIEWING FEATURES IN MICROSOFT WORD

To start, I make sure I change my document template or the Word file I am using so that my Track Changes Options look like the ones on Figures 7-1 and 7-2:

- Word 2003: Under Tools, Options, Track Changes, the selections should look exactly like on Figure 7-1

- Word 2007 and later: Under Review, Track Changes, Change Tracking Options, make your selections match Figure 7-2.

Since the default has some oddities, you might not see the edits correctly if you do not change your settings to what I have shown on Figure 7-1 (or Figure 7-2 for Word 2007).

Also, be sure you always use View, Print Layout when you view texts. Word 2003 by default opens in Reading Layout, which is not the best way to work or see edits, in my view (in fact, you can easily disable it in Tools, Options, General, by unclicking "Allow starting in Reading Layout").

Figure 7-1   Track Changes Options in Microsoft Word 2003

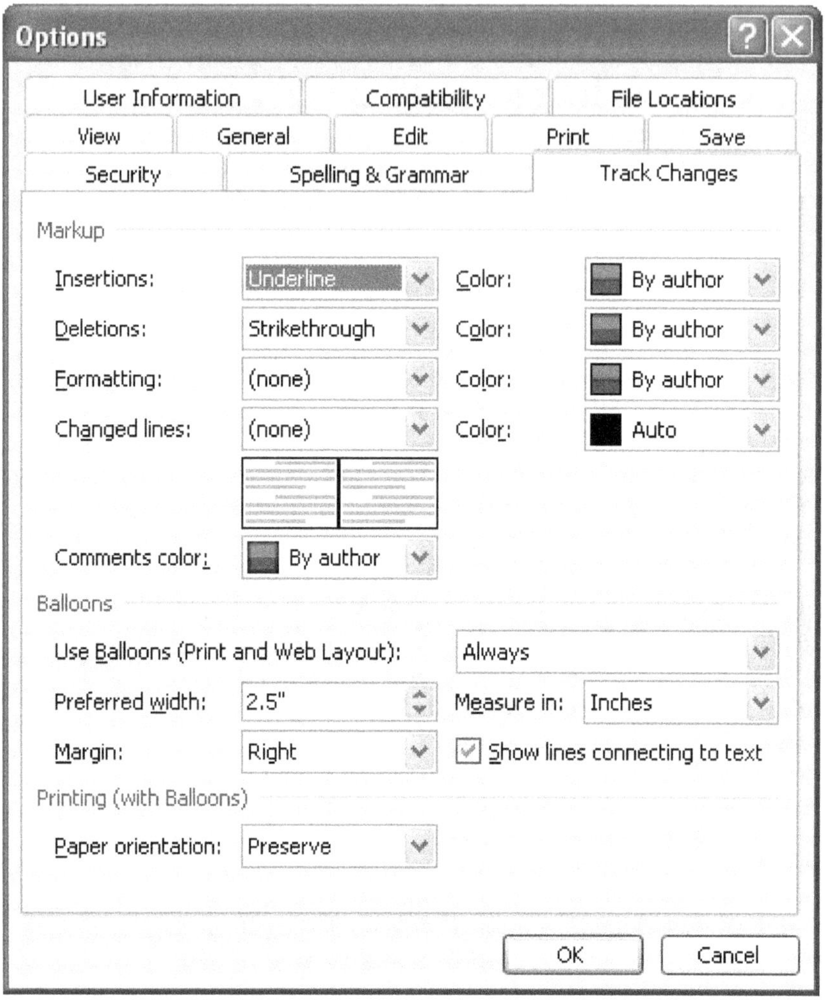

Figure 7-2   Track Changes Options in Microsoft Word 2007

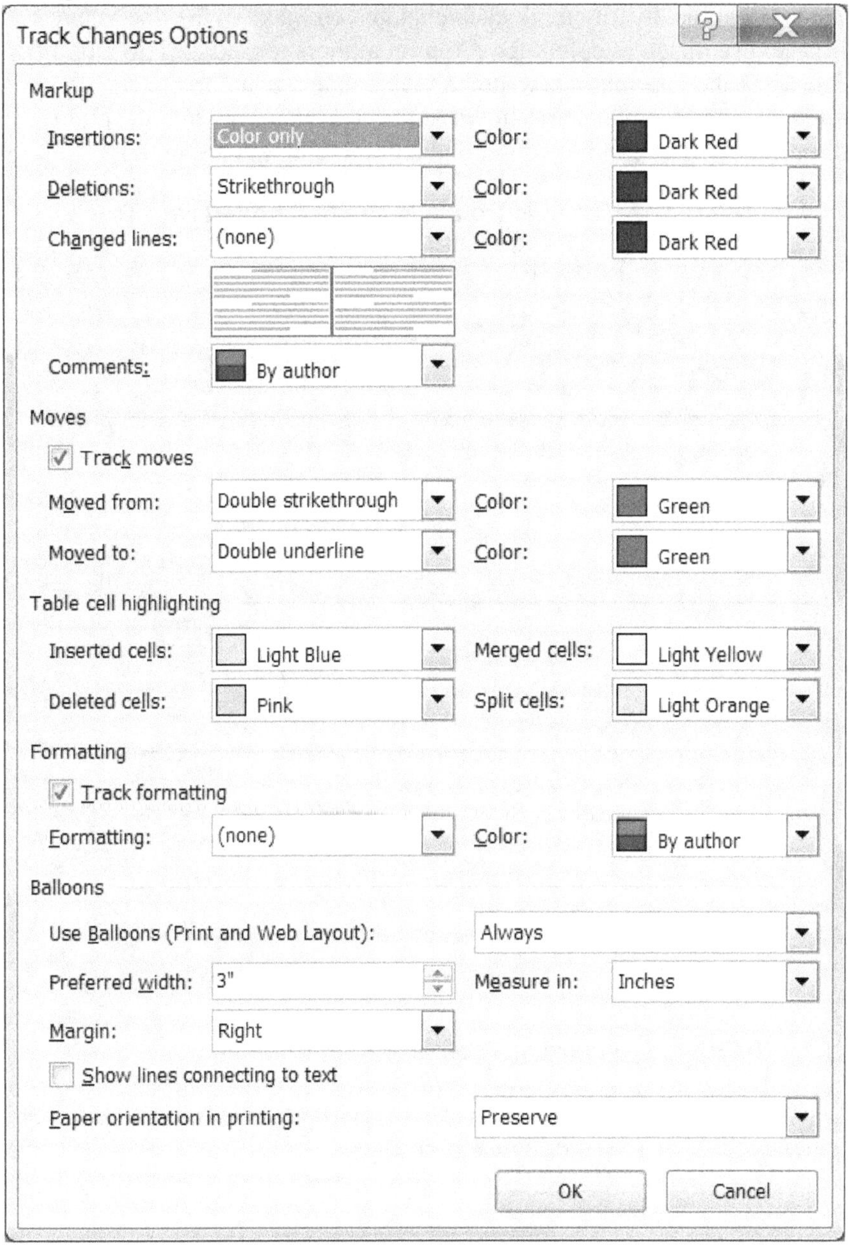

Track Changes Options

Markup

Insertions: Color only   Color: ■ Dark Red

Deletions: Strikethrough   Color: ■ Dark Red

Changed lines: (none)   Color: ■ Dark Red

Comments: ■ By author

Moves

☑ Track moves

Moved from: Double strikethrough   Color: ■ Green

Moved to: Double underline   Color: ■ Green

Table cell highlighting

Inserted cells: □ Light Blue   Merged cells: □ Light Yellow

Deleted cells: □ Pink   Split cells: □ Light Orange

Formatting

☑ Track formatting

Formatting: (none)   Color: ■ By author

Balloons

Use Balloons (Print and Web Layout):   Always

Preferred width: 3"   Measure in: Inches

Margin: Right

☐ Show lines connecting to text

Paper orientation in printing: Preserve

OK   Cancel

7.1   Using Track Changes

"Track Changes" is a feature of Word that allows each user to view comments and revisions throughout the review process. Once enabled, Word will automatically track each change you make in the document. It will also use different colors for different authors and editors (to a point). Figure 7-3 shows a major rewrite of Web site text using track changes. Deletions and comments are shown in the right margin while the main editor's changes are in blue; a second editor's changes are in red.

Figure 7-3   Example from a Web Sited Edited with Track Changes and Comments

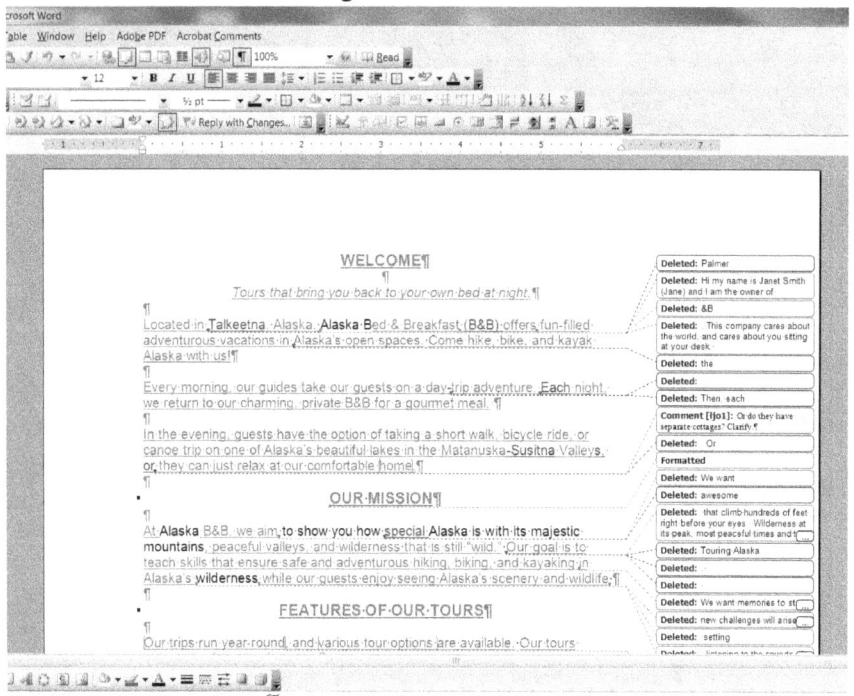

7.1.1   Using the Reviewing Toolbar

To see the reviewing toolbar, go to View, Toolbars, and be sure Reviewing is checked (see Figure 7-4).

Figure 7-4   How to Add the Reviewing Toolbar

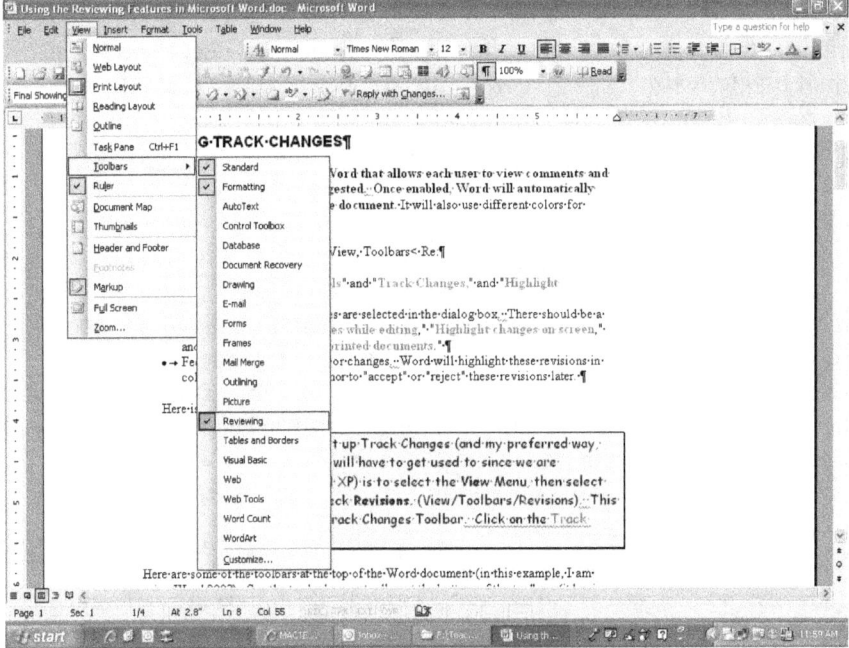

Figure 7-5 lists some of the toolbars at the top of a Word 2003 document. See the track changes toolbar at the bottom of the toolbars (it begins with "Final Showing Markup" indented from the left, then "Show."

Figure 7-5   Microsoft Word Toolbars

The bottom toolbar is the Reviewing toolbar. To the right of "Show" are the yellow boxes with blue arrows that show you how to go from comment to comment, the yellow box with the blue checkmark that allows you to accept a change or comment (or all comments if you select the dropdown arrow next to it), and the red X that allows you to delete a comment (or all comments if you select the dropdown).

7.1.2 Accepting All Changes

Important: to the right of the yellow box with the **blue checkmark** is a **small black down arrow**. Click on this to open a feature that allows you to **accept all changes in a document**. Generally, this is what you want to do once you have glanced through the editor's changes—accept all changes. (Most editors use track changes for changes they are sure of, such as mechanics and style issues. They use the "insert comments" feature for doubts.)

Note: At certain companies, to prevent the writers from having to spend too much time reviewing edits, the editor will not use track changes for the edits she is sure about such as style, grammar, punctuation, etc. This way the writer will not be distracted and will only have to look for the comments (or areas with track changes where the editor was not 100% certain of the changes). Let the editor know if you prefer to see all changes; this is up to the writer.

Then, use the blue arrows to go to the **comments,** which are different from the track changes. (You might prefer to go through and see the comments first, before accepting all changes, in case the editor has inserted comments such as "change ok?" So that you can clearly see through the track changes what the change was.)

When you receive your file back, you can either accept or reject the changes. You can read comments three ways:

1. By hovering your mouse cursor over the highlighted text if the "balloons" are not on.

2. By looking at the comments in the comment box in the right-hand margin (if the balloons are on, which they are in this document) (see Figure 7-6).

3. By looking at the comments bar at the bottom of your screen (see Figure 7-7).

Figure 7-6   Comment in Right Margin

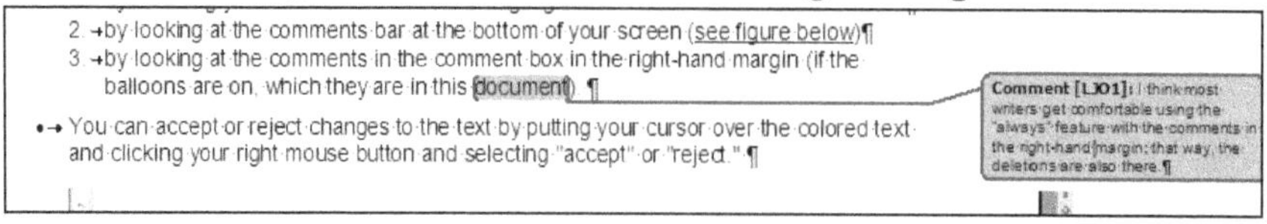

You can accept or reject changes to the text by putting your cursor over the colored text and clicking your right mouse button and selecting "accept" or "reject." You can delete the comment by clicking in the comment and then selecting the red X to delete it in the track changes toolbar.

Figure 7-7 shows how comments will be listed below the text (at the bottom of your screen) if you turn off balloons in the track changes options menu.

Figure 7-7   Comments Showing Below Document Instead of Margin

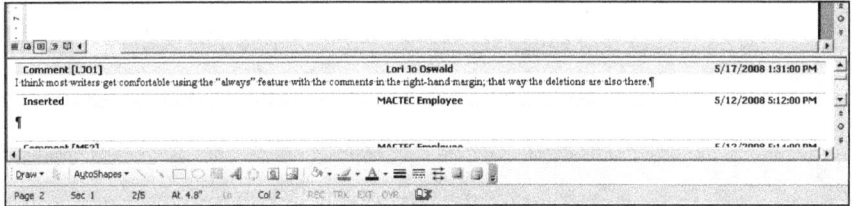

7.2   Accepting Certain Changes in Word

It might be helpful for authors to know how to accept certain changes only, so they know how to accept just my edits or formatting changes and still see the other reviewers' changes in tracked changes.

7.2.1   How to Accept Formatting Changes Only

Click the arrow to the right of Show on your reviewing toolbar (see Section 7.1.1 if you are not sure what the reviewing toolbar is), deselect everything but Formatting. Then click the arrow beside <u>Accept Change</u> and select <u>Accept All Changes Shown</u>. (Or you can hide them by just clearing Formatting from the Show menu.)

7.2.2   How to Accept Changes by One Person

Do the same process (as in Section 7.2.1) to show the edits by one person. Go to show, then reviewers, unclick all reviewers, and then just click on the ones you want to see and accept (such as Lori Jo Oswald and Eva Nagy for the technical editing). Then accept all changes shown.

7.2.3   How to Turn on Balloon Layout for Comments

Figure 7-8 is an example of two balloon comments, one from Lori Jo
(LJO1 = Lori Jo's first comment in the document), and one from an
editor with ME for initials (ME2 = ME second comment in the
document).

Figure 7-8   Balloons in Word Showing Two Commenters

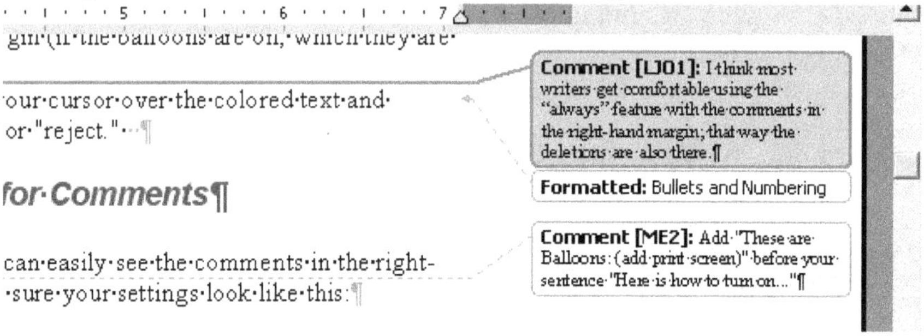

Figure 7-9 shows how to turn on the "balloons" layout option so that you
can easily see the comments in the right-hand margin. Go to Tools,
Options, Track Changes. Then make sure your settings look like this:

Figure 7-9   Turning on Balloons Layout

7.3   Using Comments

7.3.1   Comments Overview

The inserted comments are where the editor had some doubt, question, or requested more information. This is where you will want to either respond or ignore the comment, and then delete each comment (using the red "x" as described next).

To the right of the small down arrow is the yellow box with the **red "x" that allows you to delete a change or comment**. To the right of the red "x" is the yellow box that allows you to **insert comments**, and to the right of that is the **redlined track changes** box that allows you to turn on or off the track changes feature. Figure 7-5 shows the track changes toolbar from Word 2003. (In Word 2007 and later, just click the Review ribbon.)

In general, once you have the toolbar open on your screen, just click on the redlined "track changes" icon on the reviewing toolbar to begin inserting changes.

7.3.2 How to Attach Your Name to the Comments

- Since there may be several editors or reviewers inserting comments, it is important to attach your name to your comments in case the author has questions.
- To attach your name, go to "Tools" and select "Options." Choose "User Information" and fill in your name and your initials (see Figure 7-10). You will only have to do this once on your computer, but if you change computers, you will need to do it again.

Figure 7-10   Adding Your Name and Initials to Word Documents

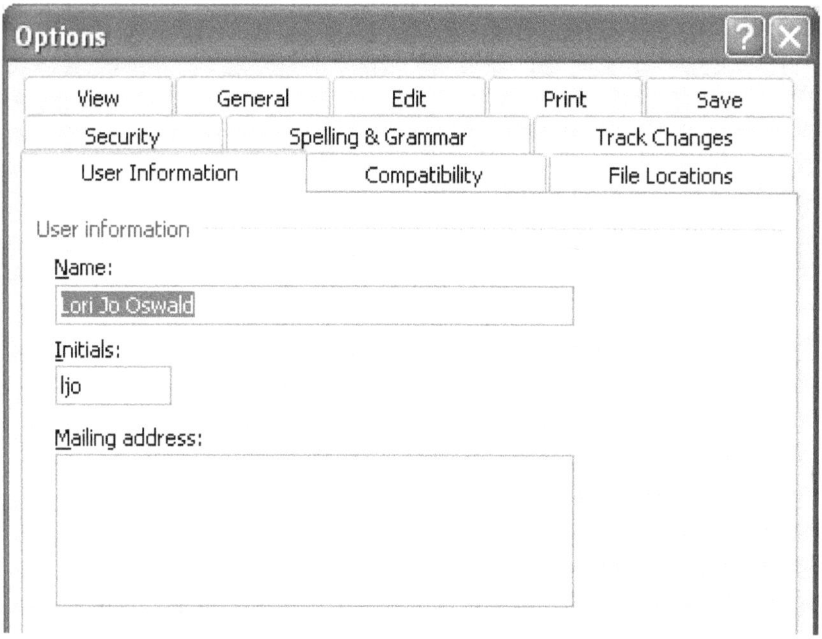

7.4   Preparing the Document for Reviewing

Make sure that you have the "Reviewing" toolbar selected so that it shows up in your toolbar. If it is not there, go to "View" and select "toolbars" and "reviewing."

To begin making comments, click on the "track changes" icon on the reviewing toolbar.

7.5   Reviewing the Document

You can now change the text directly in the document by typing or deleting and your changes will appear in color.

You can also insert a comment or question to the author by highlighting the text in question and clicking on the "Insert Comment" icon. This brings up a comment box for you to insert questions or comments.

When you actually have a comment to insert, use the yellow box (with no red or blue arrows or "x's" in it). Click the yellow box, and a comment box will be inserted at whatever point your cursor is in the text. Just type in your comment, and then click your mouse in the text to continue). Figure 7-11 is an example of a comment inserted into Word 2003:

Figure 7-11   Comment Example

Additional Information

Below is a link to a Microsoft Word training program that covers using Track Changes in Word 2003; you can Google "free training track changes in Word 2007" or whatever version you are using to find one specific to your version.
http://office.microsoft.com/training/training.aspx?AssetID=RC01160013 1033

8.0 FORMATTING AND WRITING TABLES

As with any company style, the main thing to remember with tables is to be consistent in your format. This section provides tips for formatting tables, but you might prefer a different format or shading. Still, by reading this chapter, you will understand how to make a table in Microsoft Word, and you can apply this knowledge to your own format.

8.1 Captions

The captions, or titles, of tables should be as follows:

Table 1 Title Here in Upper and Lower Case

Note the features of the above:

1. Arial 10 point bold.
2. Title in standard title case: upper and lower case.
3. Space after table title is 3 points, to separate it slightly from the table title.
4. There is no period at the end of either the table number line or the table title line.

Note that if section numbering is included instead of the 1, 2, 3, 4 format, the table and figure numbers will be different than the above example, as shown below:

Table 1-1	Title Here
Table 1-2	Title Here
Table 1-3a	Title Here
Table 1-3b	Title Here

8.2 Table Numbering

The numbering of the tables and figures should be consistent throughout the document and will depend on the numbering used in the main document.

8.2.1 Alphanumeric Numbering System

Some government agencies prefer alphanumeric numbering (I.A, I.A.1, I.A.1.a., etc.); in this case, the numbering of the table starts with the main section number where it is first mentioned in the text, followed by a period, followed by the section letter where it is first mentioned in the text (i.e., Table II.A), followed by the table number (determined by the order of the tables). Here are some examples:

- II.A-1, II.A.2, II.A-3

- III.C-1, III-C-2

The writer or editor might also choose to number related tables with an additional small letter, as follows: IV.1-9a, IV.1-9b, IV.1-9c

8.2.2 Numeric Numbering System

For the more traditional numbering system, which uses numbering only (i.e., 1.0, 1.1, 1.1.1, 1.1.1.1), the tables and figures are numbered by the section that they appear in followed by a hyphen, followed by the number (which is determined by order). Here, as an example, are the first five table numbers from Section 2.0 of a report:

Table 2-1

Table 2-2

Table 2-3

Note that for this method, the table (and figure) numbers only use two levels of numbering; it does not make a difference whether the tables appear in a first-, second-, third-, or fourth-level heading. They are still numbered in order of their textual reference. Also, no roman numerals are used. (As an example, this document uses this method for numbering sections and tables.)

8.3 Table Borders

8.3.1 Standard Borders

For most company tables, we use ½ point borders inside and outside. Some agencies or clients prefer thick borders on the outside as well as under the header row in tables:

1. For the outside border, as well as the border around the outside of the table header row(s), we use a 1½ point black border (or line).

2. For the inside of the table, we use a ¾-line border. Borders will be used around all items within a table for consistency and readability.

Table 8-1 is an example of our main borders.

Table 8-1   Standard Borders

8.3.2   *Special Column Borders*

A bolder line (1½ points) may be used between columns in one case: when there are multiple cells within a column, as in the following example (Table 8-2).

Table 8-2   Table Showing Bold Borders within Table Columns

		Title Here (Days)			Title Here (Days)			Title Here (Days)		
Title Here	Title Here	10	20	30	10	20	30	10	20	30

8.3.3   *Special Row Borders*

The heavier border (1-1/2 points) may be used between rows in one case—when subtitle rows are included (subtitle rows are described in Section 8.4.2 of this document). Note that in such a case, only the row above the subtitle row has the thicker border. See Table 8-3 for an example.

Table 8-3   Table Showing Bold Border within Table Rows

Title Here	Title Here	Title Here	Title Here	Title Here
Subtitle Here				
Subtitle Here				

8.4   Table Shading

We use shading in several ways and in several percentages, based on the area of the table the shaded areas are in, as described below:

8.4.1   Header Rows

The main use of the heading, and probably the only use for most tables, is in the header row. This is the first (top) row of the table, which sometimes includes several cells within a column. This entire area will be shaded at 15%. Table 8-4 is an example.

Table 8-4   Header Row Shading

Table 8-5 is another example, with multiple cells within a column.

Table 8-5   Multiple Cell Shading

Title Here[1]	Title Here[2]	Title Here (Days)			Title Here (Days)			Title Here (Days)		
		10	20	30	10	20	30	10	20	30

Notes:

[1] Note that the cell alignment for the far left top row is left justified, bottom of row.

[2] Note that the cell alignment for the rest of the header rows is centered, bottom of row.

8.4.2 Shaded Rows within Table Body

This section describes the two ways shading is used within a table body: for subtitle rows and long data tables.

Subtitle Rows

For tables with subtitles (i.e., subheadings) within the table body, do the following:

1. Merge the cells for the subtitle row.

2. Use Arial 10 point bold for the subtitle font.

3. Left justify the subtitle.

4. Use 10% shading for the entire row where the subtitle is.

5. Use the bolder line (1½ points) for the border above the subtitle row.

6. The paragraph spacing is 2 points above and below the text for the subtitle row, the same as the rest of the table body and header rows.

See Table 8-6 for an example.

Table 8-6 Subtitle Row Shading				
Title Here	**Title Here**	**Title Here**	**Title Here**	**Title Here**
Subtitle Here				
Subtitle Here				

8.4.3   Data Tables Longer Than One Page

For lengthy data tables (more than one page) with no subtitles, use alternating shaded lines to separate data lines from each other, as in the following example (Table 8-7). Note that the alternate shaded lines use 5% shading, but if this does not show when printed, use 10%.

Table 8-7   Shading for Data Tables Longer Than One Page

For consistency and readability, no shading should be used except for those three reasons described above.

8.5   Table Text

Table text, generally, should have the following features:

- Font—Arial, 10 points, centered, not bolded, not italicized

- Width—Table width is across the page. Margins for table and figure pages are 1 inch from top and bottom, and 1.5 inches from left and right.

- Paragraph Spacing—Table text is single space, with a 2-point space above and below the text.

- Justification—Most table text is centered, but here are exceptions:

    - Often the left-hand column and header will be left justified.

- In addition, if numbers or figures (money) with decimal places are used, the columns will be right justified, allowing just enough space from the right cell border to look balanced within the columns.

- Blank Cells—There should never be a "blank cell." Use either NA or -- to fill each cell where no data are listed. See Table 8-8 for an example.

- Cell Alignment—For the header row, align the cells at the bottom (in Microsoft Word, select the header row, right click, choose cell alignment, and choose the bottom centered tab). All rows are centered except, in some cases, the left row, which would be left justified (including the header).

- Note that no italics or all-capitalized words (except acronyms and abbreviations) are used in the table body (see Table 8-8).

Table 8-8   Sample "Blank Cell" Data and Notes

		--	NA	

Notes:
-- = No data are available for this sample.
NA = Not applicable.

A table font style with these features will be set up in the report and proposal templates for use by data processors, editors, and writers.

Exceptions: The table font size and table width can vary depending on need and text (see Section 8.6 for a discussion of table width). If, for example, it is possible to fit a table onto one page if the font size is changed to 9 points and the notes (as discussed in Section 8.7) are reduced to 8 point, the document processor has that freedom. Similarly, if the document processor needs to make the paragraph spacing above and below the table text 1 point instead of 2 to fit the table to one page, that is acceptable.

8.6   Table Width and Justification

In general, the table width is across the page.

Margins for table and figure pages are 1" from top and bottom, and 1.5" from left and right.

Exception: It is acceptable for narrow tables (for example, 2 to 3 columns with little text) to not use the entire page width. In that case, just narrow the column width to a bit wider than the text. See Table 8-9 for an example.

Table 8-9   Exception to Page Width for Tables

8.7   Table Notes

Table notes can come with three headings: Notes, Key, and Source, and if more than one is used, they should appear in that order.

Table notes have the following features:

- Arial, 9 point

- The first word (such as "Notes:" in Table 8-10, below) should have a 3-point space between it and the bottom border of the table.

- Left justified

- The words "Key:" "Notes:" and "Source:" will be bold (the colon is also bold).

- There is no border around the table notes section (see Table 8-10).

- Footnotes are included under the "Notes" heading.

- "Key" is used when acronyms and abbreviations need to be defined; the format is shown in Table 8-10.

- The words "Notes:" "Key:" and "Source:" appear on a separate line from the text that follows, as shown in Table 8-10.

- Periods are used for complete sentences and source listings.

- For acronym and abbreviation listings, no periods are used. An equal (=) sign is used between the acronym and the definition, as in GRO = gasoline range organics.

- Follow regular capitalization rules when defining acronyms and abbreviations. If the definition is capitalized (for example, EPA = Environmental Protection Agency), capitalize it in the Key section. If the definition is not usually capitalized (for example, PAH = polycyclic aromatic hydrocarbons), do not capitalize it in the Key section. (See Table 8-10.)

- Note that some clients prefer an equal sign (=) or an en dash with spaces between the abbreviation and the definition in the table notes (see Table 8-10). Personally, I prefer tabs, so if the company does not have its own style guide, I use tabs, as follows:

  USFWS   U.S. Forest Service

Table 8-10   Table Notes, Key, and Sources Example

Title Here	Title Here	Title Here (Days)	Title Here (Days)	Title Here (Days)
		23^1		
		45		
		62		

Notes:
Production and reserve data as of December 2000.
[1] Days estimated based on results from November 2001 sampling.
Key:
DRO = diesel range organics
EPA = Environmental Protection Agency
Source:
Griffiths and Gallaway (1982).

9.0 COMMONLY USED WORDS

The purpose of this section is to provide consistency with certain words. Is it one word or two? Is there a hyphen or not? Should it be capitalized or not? When in doubt, use *Merriam-Webster's Collegiate Dictionary* to be sure. Here are some examples from one company's documents:

- as-built (when used as an adjective preceding a noun, as in as-built survey)
- echo sounder (two words, Webster's)
- echo sounding (not in Webster's, but presumably two words based on echo sounder)
- fieldwork
- side-scan sonar (hyphen and use with the word sonar, Webster's)
- site-specific (adjective preceding noun)
- static GPS
- subbottom (not sub-bottom)

As you come across words that you think need to be included in this list (or changed), suggest them to the technical editor for future editions of this style guide.

Note: The words below are based on our client's preferences, Webster's, and government agency preferences, but your company may prefer a different spelling. If a word is not found in Webster's (www.m-w.com) as one word (such as streambank, which is listed here as one word because many clients prefer it that way; however, if the company does not have a preference, I will make it two words since it does appear in Webster's as one [i.e., stream bank]). But company style rules. Therefore, you may have your own preferences for some of these. Examples are wellfield (*well field* since not in dictionary, but often one word per company preference) and *work plan* (two words since not in Webster's, but many companies prefer workplan).

Note: Adjectives listed with hyphens only take the hyphen when they appear *before* the noun.

A

above grade (adverb: occurred above grade)

above ground (adverb: occurred 50 feet above ground)

abovegrade (adjective: before noun; abovegrade work)

aboveground (adjective: aboveground tank, but: pipe was located above ground)

absorption

accommodate

acrolein

across-bed

adapter (not adaptor)

adsorb (vs. absorb)

adsorption

aerial

air bag (noun)

air conditioning (noun)

airborne

air-cooled

airflow

airport

airstream

airtight

all right (incorrect: alright)

allocable

alluvial, alluvium

already, all ready

analog (a chemical compound that is structurally similar to another); otherwise, use analogue

analytes

anemometer

anion

anisotropy, anis tropic

anticline

appendices (plural)

appendix (singular)

aquifer, aquitard

areal

areawide

auger

autoignition

autorefrigeration

autotransformer

B

back draft

back pressure (not back-pressure unless adjective before noun)

back up (verb)

backfill (noun), backfilled

backflow

backhoe

backlighted

backup (noun, adjective)

backwash

backwater

back welding

backyard

baffle board

baghouse

bakehouse

bar screen

bark chips

bark dust

base flow

base map

base station

baseline

base-neutral-acid

baseplate

bases (plural of basis)

basewide

basinwide

bathymetric (adjective)
bathymetrical (adjective)
bathymetrically (adverb)
bathymetry (noun)
bay water
bedrock
behavior (not behaviour)
below grade (adverb: occurred below grade)
below ground (adverb: occurred below the ground)
below-grade (adjective or noun)
belowground (adjective: belowground sampling)
bench mark (permanent elevation marker)
benchlands
benchmark (standard; point of reference)
bench-scale
biannual (occurring twice a year)
biennial (occurring every 2 years)
biocell
biodegradeable
bioremediation
bioturbated
bioventing
biweekly
block work (construction)
blow line
blow-count (noun)
blowdown (noun, adjective)
blow down (verb)
blowup (noun, adjective); blow up (verb)
bondholder
bookkeeping
borehole

bottom-land
bottommost
break down (verb)
breakdown (noun)
breakup (noun)
build out (verb)
build up (verb)
buildout (noun)
build-up (adjective)
buildup (noun)
built-up
bulldozer
buoys
buy back (verb)
buy-back (adjective: buy-back terms)
bypass
by-product

C

caliper (not calliper)
campground
canary grass
canister (Webster's prefers to cannister)
cannot
carbureted
carryover
casthouse
cataclastic
catch basin
cation
Cenozoic era
center pivot
centerline
centigrade (international term for Celsius)
chain wheel
chain-link (adjective: chain-link fence)

chain-of-custody (adjective)
change-out
Charpy
check out (verb)
check stop
checklist
checkout (noun)
checkpoint
chipboard
citywide
clayey
claypan
claystone
clean up (verb)
cleanup (adjective/noun; cleanup equipment)
climatological
close out (verb)
closeout (adjective/noun)
close-up
coal tar
coarse-grained (adjective)
coastline
coauthor
cobbly
cocaptain
cochair
co-composting
co-containment
cofferdam
colinear
colluvium
color (not colour)
combined-sewer (adjective)
commingle
companywide
compatibility
condenser (not condensor)
connate

constant-discharge test
contaminant (noun)
contaminate (verb)
conterminous
cool down
co-own
co-owner
co-ownership
corehole
Coriolis (effect or force)
corrosion-resistant (adjective)
cost-effective (adjective)
cost-effectiveness
cost-of-service (adjective: cost-of-service fees)
coulomb
Coulomb field
Coulomb force
counter-rotate
countertop
court-ordered (adjective)
coworker
cowrite
crop out (verb)
cropland
cross connection
cross contamination
cross over (verb)
cross section
cross ties (noun)
cross-checking
crosscut
crossgradient
crossover (noun)
cross-reference
cross-sectional
curbside
cutoff (adjective: cutoff date)
cutout

D

dam site
data (plural), datum (singular)
data sets
database
datalogger
datum (singular)
dead leg
decahydration
decision maker
decision making (noun)
decision-making (adjective)
de-emphasize
deenergize
deice
deionized
-demand (peak-demand period)
-density (high-density protein)
desiccate
DEW Line
dew point
dewatered
dialogue (Webster's prefers to dialog)
dielectric
digester
dilatancy
DoD (lowercase "o")
DOE (uppercase "O")
double up
downdip
downdropping (adjective: downdropping slope)
downgradient
downhill
downhole
downslope
downspout
downstream (adjective or adverb)
downtime
drain field
drain line
drainageway
drain-down (adjective)
drainpipe
draw down (verb)
drawdown (noun)
drill bit
drill head
drill hole
drill rig
drip pan
drip-proof
drivetrain (one word if referring to automobiles; otherwise, two words)
drive-train components
drop box (noun)
drop off (verb)
drop-box (adjective: drop-box service)
drop-off (adjective: drop-off items)
dry cleaning (noun), dry-clean (verb)
dry wall
dry well
dual-phase extraction
ductwork
dump truck
dunnage
dust tight

E

earth flow
earth moving equipment
earthfill
earthwork

east side
easternmost (but east side)
echo sounder
echo sounding
ecotoxicity
ecotoxicological
electro (no hyphen or space; combine with next word, as in:)
electrohydraulic
electromelt
E-logs
e-mail
embayment
end caps (noun)
end point
end product
end result
end seal
ensure
errata
erratum
Ethernet
evapotranspiration
ex situ (no hyphen or italics)
exceedance (not exceedence)
-exempt (tax-exempt bond)
explosionproof
extra-capacity (adjective: extra-capacity trunks)
Extranet

F
facies (noun singular and plural)
fail-safe (adjective/noun)
falling-head test
fallout
farmland
fast track (noun)
fast-track (adjective)
fatal-flaw (adjective: fatal-flaw

analysis)
feasibility
federal
-feed (center-feed clarifier; step-feed mode)
feed line
feed well
feedstock
feedwater
fence line
fence post
fiberglass
field crew
field screening techniques
field streaming
field worker
fieldbus
field-wide
fieldwork (noun)
fine-grained (adjective)
fine-tune
fire chief
fire control
fire department
fire drill
fire escape
fire extinguisher
fire fighting (noun)
fire pump
fire screen
fire station
fire truck
firebox
firedamp
firefighter, fireman
fire-fighting (adjective)
firefighting (verb)
firehouse
fireman

fireplug
fireproof
firesafe
firewall
firewater
firework
firmwide
fish (for plural)
fish screen
fishkill
flame ionization
flare up (verb)
flareup (adjective/noun)
flash point
flip chart
flood way
floodplain
floodwater
floor plate
floppy disk
-flow (restricted-flow issues; on-flow train)
flow line
flow path
flow rate
flow sheet
flow stream
flow top
flowchart
flowmeter
fluoride
fluvial
fly ash
-focus (deep-focus earthquake)
focused (not focussed)
follow up (verb)
follow-up (noun/adjective)
food chain
force main

forego
foregoing
forklift
formwork (construction)
fossiliferous (adjective)
freestanding
freezeback
Freon
fresh water (noun)
freshwater (adjective)
friable
front loader
front yard
front-end loader
fulfill (not fulfil)
full time (noun)
full-time (adjective: full-time equivalent)
furans
fuse holder
FY 99, FY 00

G

gas station
gas-oil (mixture)
gauge (not gage)
gauge line
gauss
gearbox
geochemical
geodetic
geologic (except U.S. Geological Survey)
geomembrane
geomorphic
Geo-probe
geotechnical
geotextile
giveaway
-glass (cast-glass ceramics)

glass-ceramic (noun and adjective)
gneissic
-grade (at-grade floor)
-graded (well-graded roadway)
grain-size analysis
grassland
grasslike
gray (not grey)
green chain
-grid (coarse-grid receptor)
gridded
ground bed
ground cover
groundwater (except National Ground Water Association) (but note: surface water)

H
half-life (noun)
halocarbons
halogen
hand out (verb)
hand switch
handheld
handhold
handhole
handout (noun)
hands-on
hard copy
hard hat
head loss
head shaft
headspace
headwall
headworks
heterogeneity
high resistivity (adjective)
high-capacity production
high-level (adjective)

hillslope
HNu (brand name, portable)
hold-down (tanks)
holding time (not hold time)
holdup (delay)
hollow-stem (adjective)
Holocene
homeowner
homogeneous, homogeneity
hook hole
hookup
horsepower
hot spot
hydro (note: no hyphen after hydro)
hydrogeology, hydrogeologic
hydropower
HydroPunch (but lowercase if generic)
hydrotest

I
ice floes
in depth (adverb: studied in depth)
in situ (no hyphen or italics)
inboard (adjective)
in-board (adjective: in-board motor)
incompatibility
in-county (adjective: in-county use)
in-depth (adjective: in-depth evaluation)
inflow (noun)
inhomogeneous
in-house (adjective: in-house distribution)
in-line (adjective: in-line service)

in-place (adjective: in-place test)
in-plant (adjective: in-plant operations)
in-service (adjective: in-service testing)
installation-wide
in-stream
interbred, interbredded
interdisciplinary
interfinger
interlayered
intermittent
intermodular
Internet
ion exchange
isoctane
isotropic
iterative

J
job site
judgment
juxtapose

K
Kelvin
kerosine (component of jet fuel)
keylock
kick off (verb)
kickoff (noun)
Kjeldahl
kriging

L
label, labeled, labeling
lamina (noun singular), laminae (plural)
land clearing
landfarm
landfill (noun)

landform
landowner
landslide
land-spreading (adjective)
land-take (adjective as in land-take requirements)
large-scale
lay-up
leach field
leach line
leachate
leak-proof
leak-tight
least squares (noun plural)
leftover
-level (low-level radiation)
life cycle (noun)
life raft
life span
life-cycle (adjective preceding noun)
lignin
-like (only if preceded by double 11:likelihood
line pipe
line shaft
lineal
linear
liquefaction
lithologic (adjective)
load out (verb)
-loading (barge-loading facility)
load-out (adjective)
lockdown
lockset
logbook
lognormal (adjective)
long range (noun)
long term (adverb/noun)

long-range (adjective)
long-standing
long-term (adjective)
low-capacity tank
lowlands
low-lying (adjective)
low-permeability (adjective)
low-resistivity (adjective)
low-yield
lunch room
lysimeter

M
main line
mainframe
make up (verb)
makeup (noun and adjective)
-making (steel-making process)
man-day (use workday)
manganese
manlift
man-made
maplet
medium (noun singular), media (noun plural)
medium-grained (adjective)
medium-range missile
medium-sized
megascopic
meltwater
mesic
metasediments
meter (not metre)
Method Three (not Method 3)
micaceous (adjective)
microcomputer
micromho(s)
microorganism
microwell
midpoint

milestone
mill water
millscale
minimize (not minimise)
modeling (not modelling)
moistureproof
monitoring well
mudflow
multi (no hyphen; join with next word)
multibeam
multidisciplinary
multifamily residence
multilayered
multimedia
multipathway
multiphase
multitask
multiyear

N
nameplate
naphtha
nationwide
no-action (adjective: no-action alternative)
no-build (adjective: no-build alternative)
nonconductive
non-debt-funded (adjective: non-debt-funded project)
nondetect
nonequilibrium
nonhazardous
nonlisted
nonmarine
nonroutine
non-steady-state (adjective: non-steady-state issues)
nontoxic

nonturbid
nonvolatile
non-water-bearing
nonwettable
northernmost
northwest-southeast
northwest-trending
N-value (noun)

O
obturator
occur/occurred/occurrence
off-gas
off-line
off-load
off-loading
off-peak (adjective)
off-post or off post
off-road (adjective: off-road vehicle)
offset (noun, adjective, or verb)
offshore
off-site (adjective and adverb)
off-take (point)
oil field
oil rig
oil well
oilless
on line (in or into operation)
ongoing
on-line (adjective or adverb)
on-post or on post
onshore
on-site (adjective or adverb)
orthoclay
orthophosphate
Otto fuel (not auto)
outbuildings
outcrop (noun/verb)
outfall

output
outsource
overburden
overflow
overlap
overlie, overlay, overlain
overrun
overwinter

P
packer test, packer-tested
panelboard
parametric
parkland
part-time (adjective)
pass through (verb)
pass-through (noun)
pastureland
pebble-sized
penetrameter
per person (adjective: per person data)
per se (no hyphen or italic)
percent
percent (usually no % except in figures/tables; however, this can vary per company style)
permeability, permeable
persistent
petroleum hydrocarbon-contaminated soils
pH
phase in (verb)
phase out (verb)
phase-in (adjective)
phase-out (adjective)
phenol
photoionization
phreactic
physiography

piezometer, piezometric
pillow block
pilot-scale
pipe lay (if an adjective before a
noun, use pipe-lay)
pipe mill
pipe rack
pipe wall
pipefitting
pipeline
pipework
pitot tube
plan holder
plasterboard
playground
Pleistocene
pole yard
policyholder
policymaker
policy-making
polyethylene
polyurethane
pore water
portland cement
postaccident (adjective:
postaccident data)
post-closure
post-evalution
postmortem (adjective /noun)
posttreatment (adjective)
pot room
pothole
potliner
power line
power pack
power plant
powerhouse
powerstation
practice

pre (generally no hyphen with
pre; see Webster's to be sure)
precede
precursor
predominant (adjective)
predominate (verb)
preestablished
preevaluation
preexisting
preplanned
pressure meter
pretreatment
preventive (not preventative)
principal-in-charge
print out (verb)
printout (noun; adjective)
problem solving (noun)
process area
process water
procure/procured/procuring
project-specific (adjective)
promontory
proof-roll
propellant
pseudoclassical
pull box
pullout
pump house
pump out (verb)
pump station
pump-out (adjective before
noun)
punch list
purge-and-trap method
push-button

Q

quack grass
quantitation
quartzose (adjective)

quasi-permanent

R

radii (plural of radius)
radioactive
rail yard
railcar
railroad
railroad tracks
rain gear
rainfall
rainwater
rangeland
-rate (constant-rate test)
rate setting (noun)
ratemaking
ratepayer
read out (verb)
readout (noun)
real-time
real-time kinematic
reconnaissance
record keeping (noun)
record-keeping (adjective)
re-create (verb; to create again)
-reducing (cost-reducing measures)
reed canary grass
reequilibrated
reestablish
reevaluate
reexamine
regarding or in regard to (not in regards to)
-regulating (temperature-regulating valves)
reinstall
-related (hazardous-waste-related tasks)
remediation

reprint
reproducibility, reproducible
-resistant (corrosion-resistant metal)
resistivity
restroom
re-treat (to treat again)
re-use (adjective, as in re-use planning)
reuse (verb)
right-of-way
rinsate (not rinseate)
rinse water
riprap
riverbank
riverbed
road map
roadbed
roadway
rock fill
rockfall
roll off (verb)
roll up (verb)
-rolled (hot-rolled steel)
roll-off (adjective: roll-off box)
roll-up (adjective: roll-up shades)
-roof (flat-roof building)
rooftop (adjective: rooftop repairs)
rule making (noun)
rule-making (adjective)
rule set
run off (verb)
run on (verb)
run out (verb); run-out (noun)
runoff (noun/adjective)
run-on (adjective /noun)
run-out (noun); run out (verb)

S

salt water (noun)
saltwater (adjective)
sandbag
sandbank
sandblasting, grit
sandpack
sandpaper
-scale (large-scale operations)
scale up (verb)
scaleup (adjective /noun)
scrap yard
seawater
sedimentary
selenium
self-contained
self-feeder
self-monitoring (adjective)
semiannual
semiarid
semiconfined
semilog, semilogarithmic
semivolatile
set aside (verb)
set point
set up (verb)
set-aside (noun)
-setting, (rate-setting goals)
setup (noun)
sewer flow
sewer shed
sewerline
sheepsfoot
sheet iron
sheet metal
sheet metalwork
sheet piles
sheet steel
sheet tin

Sheetrock®
shell-like (but grasslike; check Webster's to be sure)
shipyard
shop blast
shoreline
short range (noun)
short term (adverb/noun)
short-range (adjective)
short-term (adjective)
shut down (verb)
shut off (verb)
shutdown (noun)
shutdown valve
shut-in
shutoff (adjective)
side boom
side slope
side water
side-scan sonar
siliceous
siltstone
single-family residence
single-phase (adjective)
site work
site-specific (adjective: site-specific issue)
sitewide
sledgehammer
-slope (down-slope length)
slug catcher (some companies prefer one word)
smooth sheet
smoothed-in (adjective: smoothed-in roadbed)
snakebite
snowmelt
soil gas (soil gas field survey)
soil-pore liquid

solenoid
solenoid valve
solid waste
sonar
sonication
-source (near-source well)
southernmost
southwest-northeast
southwest-trending
spark-proof
spectrometry,
spectrophotometry
split case
split-spoon sampler
-spoon (split-spoon sample)
spray head
spreadsheet
spring line
stainless steel (noun)
stainless-steel (adjective)
stand-alone (adjective stand-alone document)
standby
stand-off
standpipe
start up (verb)
start-up (adjective/noun)
state of the art (noun)
state-certified
state-of-the-art (adjective)
statewide
static GPS
-status (special-status species)
steady state (noun/adjective)
steam clean (verb)
steam generator
steel making (noun)
steel-making (adjective)
-stem (hollow-stem auger)

step-discharge test
step-down, step-up (noun/adjective)
step-drawdown test
stepwise
stop nut
storativity
storm water (noun)
straightforward
stratigraphy, stratigraphic
stream water
streambank
streambed
streamflow
strength (full-strength test)
stubout (adjective/noun)
sub (generally no hyphen; check Webster's to be sure)
subaerial
subarea
subbasin
subbottom
subcontractor
subsea
subsection
subsurface
subsystem
sulfate, sulfite, sulfitic
sulfur
sulfur, sulfuric, sulfurous
Super Sacks
Superfund
supernate
supersede (not supercede)
surface water
surficial
switch ties
switchgrass
switchyard

syncline, synclinal

T

tailwater

take off (verb)

takeoff (noun/adjective)

talus

tamper-proof

tamper-resistant

tank farm

tannin

tare

task force

task order

teamwork (noun)

tectonic

Teflon® (trademark)

telltale (a type of valve)

test pit

-tested (tightness-tested seal)

through bolt

time frame

time line

time sheet

time-consuming

timeframe

timetable

toolshed

top-of-casing (adjective)

topsoil

total Kjeldahl nitrogen

touch-up

toward (not towards)

-track (fast-track schedule)

trade name

trademark

tradeoff

trans-Alaska oil pipeline (AP style)

Trans-Alaska Pipeline System

(TAPS) (Alyeska style)

transfer/transferring/transferred/ transferable/transferal

transmissivity

travel, traveled, traveling

-treated (heat-treated metals)

tremie (adjective, not verb)

trench side

troubleshooting

trunk line

trunnion

truss-joist

t-test

tubesheet

tuffaceous

turbid

turbidity

turbulent (not turbulant)

turnaround

turnaround time

turndown

twofold

two-phased (adjective)

Tyrek®

U

U.S. (not US, and never define U.S.)

U.S.C. (for U.S. Code)

ullage

ultra-high (adjective: ultra-high frequency)

ultraviolet

unconfined

unconformable, unconformity

unconsolidated

under floor (adverb: the mouse was under the floor)

under ground (adverb: the pipe was under the ground)

under water (adverb: the site was under water)

under way (adverb)

undercut

underdeposit

underdraln

underfloor (adjective: underfloor pipe)

underflow

underground (adjective: underground pipe)

underlie, underlay, underlain

underlying

underrun

under-voltage

underwater (adjective: underwater activity)

underway (adjective) (occurring, performed, or used while traveling or in motion: underway replenishment of fuel)

United States (noun), U.S. (adjective)

unsaturated

unthreaded

upbed

updip

upflow

upgradient (adjective: upgradient well)

uphill

uplands

uppermost

uptake

upwind

usable (not useable)

EPA-approved

user friendly

V

vadose zone

Vendor

venturi

Visqueen® (not Visquine)

volatile

volumetric

W

walk through (verb)

walk-through (noun)

-wall (double-wall construction)

wallboard

wash wastes

wash water

washout

waste line

waste load

waste stream

wastewater

water body

water main

water spray

water stop

water table

water well

water-bearing (adjective)

water-bearing unit (modifier)

water-cooled (adjective)

watercourse

waterflood

waterfowl

waterline

waterpower

watershed

watertight

waterwash

waterway

Web site

weekday

weep holes

weldability
weld pack
-well (near-well transmissivity)
well bay
well house
well line
well pad
well point
well screen
well work
wellbore
wellfield
wellhead
well-known (adjective before noun)
well known (after noun)
wellpoint
wellsite
west side
westernmost (but west side)
wet well
wheatgrass
wholly owned
wind up (verb)
windblown
windbreak
windrow (row of heaped matter)
windup (adjective/noun)
wingwall
wireway
wood waste
wood yard
work area
work over (transitive verb; to work over something)
work plan
work scope
work sheet
work site

workday
workers' compensation
workflow
workforce
workload
workman
workover (adjective, as in a hydraulic workover rig)
workplace
workshop
workstation
workweek
worldwide
worst-case scenario
w-test

Y

yard—see backyard, front yard, pole yard, rail yard, shipyard, scrap yard, switchyard, and wood yard
yearlong (adjective)
year-round (adjective)

Z

-zone (trench-zone data

10.0 COMMONLY MISSPELLED WORDS

absence
abundance
accessible
accidentally
acclaim
accommodate
accomplish
accordion
accumulate
achievement
acquaintance
across
address
advertisement
aggravate
alleged
annual
apparent
appearance
argument
atheist
athletics
attendance
auxiliary
balloon
barbecue
barbiturate
bargain
basically
beggar
beginning
believe
biscuit

bouillon
boundary
Britain
business
calendar
camouflage
cantaloupe
category
cemetery
chagrined
challenge
characteristic
changing
chief
cigarette
climbed
collectible
colonel
colossal
column
coming
committee
commitment
comparative
competent
completely
concede
conceive
condemn
conscientious
consciousness
consistent
continuous

controlled

coolly

corollary

convenient

correlate

correspondence

counselor

courteous

courtesy

criticize

deceive

defendant

deferred

dependent

descend

description

desirable

despair

desperate

develop

development

difference

dilemma

dining

disappearance

disappoint

disastrous

discipline

disease

dispensable

dissatisfied

dominant

drunkenness

easily

ecstasy

efficiency

eighth

either

eligible

emperor

enemy

entirely

equipped

equivalent

escape

especially

exaggerate

exceed

excellence

excellent

exhaust

existence

expense

experience

experiment

explanation

extremely

exuberance

fallacious

fallacy

familiar

fascinate

feasible

February

fictitious

finally

financially

forcibly

foreign

forfeit

formerly

foresee

forty

fourth

fulfill

fundamentally

gauge

generally

genius
government
governor
grievous
guarantee
guerrilla
guidance
handkerchief
happily
harass
height
heinous
hemorrhage
heroes
hesitancy
hindrance
hoarse
hoping
humorous
hypocrisy
hypocrite
ideally
idiosyncrasy
ignorance
imaginary
immediately
implement
incidentally
incredible
independence
independent
indicted
indispensable
inevitable
influential
information
inoculate
insurance
intelligence

intercede
interference
interpret
interrupt
introduce
irrelevant
irresistible
island
jealousy
jewelry
judicial
knowledge
laboratory
legitimate
leisure
length
lenient
license
lieutenant
lightning
likelihood
likely
loneliness
losing
lovely
luxury
magazine
maintain
maintenance
manageable
maneuver
marriage
mathematics
medicine
millennium
millionaire
miniature
minutes
mischievous

missile	parallel
misspelled	parliament
mortgage	particularly
mosquito	pavilion
mosquitoes	peaceable
murmur	peculiar
muscle	penetrate
mysterious	perceive
narrative	performance
naturally	permanent
necessary	permissible
necessity	permitted
neighbor	perseverance
neutron	persistence
ninety	physical
ninth	physician
noticeable	picnicking
nowadays	piece
nuisance	pilgrimage
obedience	pitiful
obstacle	planning
occasion	pleasant
occasionally	portray
occurred	possess
occurrence	possessive
official	potato
omission	potatoes
omit	practically
omitted	prairie
opinion	preference
opponent	preferred
opportunity	prejudice
oppression	preparation
optimism	prescription
ordinarily	prevalent
origin	primitive
outrageous	privilege
overrun	probably
panicky	procedure

proceed
professor
prominent
pronounce
pronunciation
propaganda
psychology
publicly
pursue
quandary
quarantine
questionnaire
quizzes
realistically
realize
really
recede
receipt
receive
recognize
recommend
reference
referred
relevant
relieving
religious
remembrance
reminiscence
repetition
representative
resemblance
reservoir
resistance
restaurant
rheumatism
rhythm
rhythmical
roommate
sacrilegious

sacrifice
safety
salary
satellite
scenery
schedule
secede
secretary
seize
separate
sergeant
several
shepherd
shining
similar
simile
simply
sincerely
skeptic
skeptical
skiing
soliloquy
sophomore
souvenir
specifically
specimen
sponsor
spontaneous
statistics
stopped
strategy
strength
strenuous
stubbornness
subordinate
subtle
succeed
success
succession

sufficient	transferred
supersede	truly
suppress	twelfth
surprise	tyranny
surround	unanimous
susceptible	undoubtedly
suspicious	unnecessary
syllable	until
symmetrical	usage
synonymous	usually
tangible	vacuum
technical	valuable
technique	vengeance
temperature	vigilant
tendency	village
themselves	villain
theories	violence
therefore	visible
thorough	warrant
though	Wednesday
through	weird
till	wherever
tomorrow	wholly
tournament	yacht
tourniquet	yield
tragedy	zoology

11.0   COMMONLY CONFUSED WORDS

Any handbook such as those used in college English courses should suffice to answer most English usage questions. Still, the most common errors are included here for your reference and for clarification. (Sources include *The St. Martin's Handbook* and *The Simon & Schuster Handbook for Writers*, as well as from my own experience editing and teaching.)

a, an. Use "a" with a word that begins with a consonant (a forest), with a sounded h (a hemisphere, a history), or with another consonant sound such as "you" or "wh" (a euphoric moment, a one-sided match, a 1,000-gallon tank). Use "an" with a word that begins with a vowel (an umbrella), with a silent h (an honor), or with a vowel sound (an X-ray). (I often see writers get confused by the "h" rule and write "an history," for example; the test is if it's a sounded h, use "a" not "an.")

accept, except. The verb accept means "receive" or "agree to." *Melanie will accept the job offer.* The preposition except means "aside from" or "excluding." *All the plaintiffs except Mr. Smith decided to accept the settlement offered by the defendant.*

absorption, adsorption. Absorption means to soak up, like a sponge; dissolving in liquid or gas. Adsorption refers to when one entity adheres to another, as in carbon adsorption, where a molecule adheres to the activated carbon surface.

advice, advise. Advice is a noun meaning opinion or suggestion; advise is a verb meaning offer or provide advice. *Jenna advised Sally that Frank's advice was poor.*

affect, effect. Affect is a verb meaning influence or move the emotions of. Effect is a noun meaning result, or, less commonly, a verb meaning bring about. Use the "the" test. If you can put "the" in front of it, you have a noun and effect. *The effect of the rain was a flood.* If "the" can only go after the word, use affect, as in: *The rain affected the roof by causing it to break.*

all ready, already. All ready means fully prepared. Already means previously. We were all ready for Lucy's party when we learned that she had already left.

all right. Always write "all right" as two words.

a lot. A lot is always two words. Avoid in formal (i.e., technical) writing.

a.m., p.m. Use only with numbers, not as substitutes for the words morning, afternoon, or evening.

among, between. Use between for two items or people and among for three or more items or people. *The relationship between the twins is different front that among the other three children.*

amount, number. Use amount for quantities that you cannot count (singular nouns such as water, light, or power). Use number for quantities that you can count (usually plural nouns such as objects or people). *A small number of volunteers cleared a large amount of brush within a few hours.*

and/or. Avoid if possible. Use x, y, or both instead.(I generally try to avoid the slash because it is confusing and seems like lazy writing.)

anion, cation. Anion is an ion with a negative charge; cation is an ion with a positive charge.

any body, anybody, any one, anyone. Note the differences: *Although anyone could enjoy carving wood, not just anybody could make a sculpture like that. Any body of water has its own distinctive ecology. Customers were allowed to buy only two sale items at any one time.*

anyway, anyways. Use anyway, never anyways.

as, because. Avoid using "as" for "because" or when in sentences where its meaning is not clear. For example, does *Carl left town as his father was arriving* mean at the same time as his father was arriving or because his father was arriving?

as, like, such as. For comparisons, use "as" when comparing two qualities that people or objects possess. *The box is as wide as it is long.* Also use "as" to identify equivalent terms in a description. *Gary served as moderator at the town meeting.* Use "like" to indicate similarity but not equivalency: *Hugo, like Jane, was a detailed observer.* In formal writing, "such as" is preferable to "like" in most cases.

assure, ensure, insure. Assure means convince or promise, and its direct object is usually a person or persons. *The candidate assured the voters he would not raise taxes.* Ensure and insure both mean make certain, but insure is usually used in the specialized sense of protection against financial loss. *When the city began water rationing to ensure that the supply would last, the Browns found that they could no longer afford to insure their car wash business.* (Note that some companies avoid using "ensure" as it promises too much: *We will ensure that the site is cleaned up by May 15, 2015.*)

as to. Do not use as to as a substitute for about. *Connie was unsure about* (not as to) *David's intentions.*

because of, due to. Both phrases are used to describe the relationship between a cause and an effect. Use due to when the effect (a noun) is stated first and followed by the verb to be. *His illness was due to malnutrition.* (Illness, a noun, is the effect.) Use because of, not due to, when the effect is a clause, not a noun. *He was sick because of malnutrition.* (He was sick, a clause, is the effect.)

being as, being that. Avoid these expressions (substitutes for because) in formal writing.

beside, besides. Beside, a preposition, means next to. Besides is either a preposition meaning other than or in addition to or an adverb meaning moreover. *No one besides Elaine knows whether the tree is still growing beside the house.*

bi, semi. Bi means every other, and semi means twice in a given period.

breath, breathe. Breath is the noun, and breathe is the verb.

but, yet, however. Use these words separately, not together.

but that, but what. Avoid these as substitutes for that.

can, may. Can refers to ability and may to possibility or permission to do something. *Since I can ski the slalom well, I may win the race. May I leave early to practice?*

can't, couldn't. Avoid all contractions in formal writing.

choose, chose. Choose is the simple form of the verb; chose is the past-tense form. *I chose the movie last week, so you choose it tonight.*

compare to, compare with. Compare to means describe one thing as similar to another. *Juanita compared the noise to the roar of a waterfall.* Compare with is the more general activity of noting similarities and differences between objects or people. *The detective compared the latest photograph with the old one, noting how the man's appearance had changed.*

complement, compliment. Complement means go well with or enhance. Compliment means praise.

comprise, compose. Comprise means contain (the whole comprises the parts). Compose means make up (the parts compose the whole). *The class comprises 20 students. Twenty students compose the class.*

consequently, subsequently. Consequently means as a result or therefore. Subsequently just means afterwards. Roger lost his job, and subsequently I lost mine. Consequently, I was unable to pay my rent.

continual, continuous. Continual describes an activity that is repeated at regular or frequent intervals. Continuous describes either an activity that is ongoing without interruption or an object that is connected without break. *The damage done by continuous erosion was increased by the continual storms.*

couple of. Avoid in formal writing. Say specifically what you mean.

criteria, criterion. Criterion means a standard of judgment or a necessary qualification. Criteria is the plural form.

data. The word data is the plural form of the Latin word datum, meaning a fact or a result collected during research. Treat data as plural in formal writing. *These data indicate that fewer people smoke today than 10 years ago.*

different from, different than. Different from is generally preferred in formal writing.

discreet, discrete. Discreet means tactful or prudent. Discrete means distinct or separate. *The dean's discreet encouragement brought representatives of all the discrete factions to the meeting.*

dispose, dispose of. Dispose means to incline or to be inclined toward something. Dispose of means to throw away.

disinterested, uninterested. Disinterested means unbiased or impartial. Uninterested means not interested or indifferent.

elicit, illicit. The verb elicit means to draw out or evoke. The adjective illicit means illegal.

especially, specially. Especially means very or particularly. Specially means for a special reason or purpose. *The audience especially enjoyed the new composition, specially written for the holiday.*

every day, everyday. Everyday is an adjective used to describe something as ordinary or common. Every day is an adjective modifying a noun, specifying which particular day. I ride the subway every day even though pushing and shoving are everyday occurrences.

every one, everyone. Everyone is an indefinite pronoun; every one is a noun modified by an adjective, referring to each member of a group. Because he began the assignment after everyone else, David knew that he could finish every one of the selections.

explicit, implicit. Explicit means directly or openly expressed. Implicit means indirectly expressed or implied. *The explicit message of the advertisement urged consumers to buy the product while the implicit message promised popularity.*

farther, further. Farther refers to physical distance. *How much farther is it to the jobsite?* Further refers to time or degree. *I want to avoid further delays and further misunderstandings.*

fewer, less. Use fewer with objects or people that can be counted (plural nouns). Use less with amounts that cannot be counted (singular nouns). *The world would be safer with fewer bombs and less* *hostility.*

firstly, secondly, thirdly. These are old-fashioned for introducing a series of points. Use first, second, and third.

following. Following is an adjective (the following items) or a noun (a large following), not a substitute for after. *After the holes were dug*, not *Following the hole digging.*

from . . . to, between . . . and. These have different meanings. *The store operated from 1950 to 1970.* This means the store was open from the year 1950 to the year 1970. *The store operated between 1950 and 1970.* This means the store was open from 1951 to 1969. *Concentrations were detected from 5 mg/kg to 10 mg/kg.* The concentrations, in this case, were from 5 mg/kg to 10 mg/kg. *Concentrations detected were between 5 mg/kg and 100 mg/kg.* In this case, the concentrations were from 6 (or 5.1 . . . anything higher than 5) mg/kg to 99 (or 99.9 . . . anything lower than 100) mg/kg.

good, well. Good is an adjective and should not be used as a substitute for the adverb well. Gabriel is a good host who cooks quite well.

has got to, has to. Avoid these colloquial phrases for must.

have, of. *Have*, not *of*, should follow could, would, should, or might.

he/she, his/her. He/she and his/her are ungainly ways to avoid sexism in writing. Other solutions are to write out *he or she* or to alternate using *he* and *she*. But perhaps the best solution is the eliminate the pronouns entirely or to make the subject plural (they), thereby avoiding all reference to gender. *Everyone should carry his or her driver's license with him or her* could be revised to *Drivers should carry driver's licenses at all times* or to *People should carry their driver's licenses with them.*

hopefully. Hopefully is widely misused to mean it is hoped, but its correct meaning is with hope. Sam watched the roulette wheel hopefully, not Hopefully, Sam will win.

if, whether. Use whether or whether or not (I prefer to just use "whether" without the "or not") to express an alternative. *She was considering whether to buy the new software.* Reserve if for the subjunctive case. *If it should rain tomorrow, our class will meet in the gym.*

impact. As a noun, impact means a forceful collision. As a verb, impact means pack together. *Because they were impacted, Jason's wisdom teeth needed to be removed.* Avoid the colloquial use of impact as a vague word meaning to affect. *Population control may reduce* (not impact) *world hunger.* (Note: I see "impact" used frequently by my clients when "affected" would probably be a better choice such as "the area will not be impacted by construction"; since it is so commonly used and seems to have become acceptable for such use, I often leave as is. Here is a typical example: *To determine the extent of petroleum-hydrocarbon impacted soils in the areas of confirmed impact. . .*

imply, infer. To imply is to suggest. To infer is to make an educated guess. Speakers and writers imply; listeners and readers infer. *Beth and Peter's letter implied that they were planning a very small wedding; we inferred that we would not be invited.*

inside, inside of, outside, outside of. Drop of after the prepositions inside and outside. The class regularly met outside the building.

interact with, interface with. Avoid these colloquial expressions.

irregardless, regardless. Regardless is the correct word; irregardless is a double negative.

is when, is where. These vague and faulty shortcuts should be avoided in definitions. *Schizophrenia is a psychotic condition in which* (not when or where) *a person withdraws from reality.*

its, it's. Its is a possessive pronoun, even though it does not have an apostrophe. It's is a contraction for it is; avoid it's and other contractions in formal writing.

lay, lie. Lay means place or put. Its forms are lay, laid, laying, laid, and laid. It generally has a direct object, specifying what has been placed. *She laid her books on the desk.* Lie means recline or be positioned and does not take a direct object. Its forms are lie, lay, lain, lying. *She lay awake until 2 a.m., worrying about the exam.* Funny (and true) story: I was showing a friend of mine how well trained my dog was. I said, "Lay down," and she did not move. My friend said, "Well of course she's not moving; you are using incorrect grammar. You should have said lie down!" He was right, of course. Another incorrect example: In the song "Lay Lady Lay," the phrase "Lay across my big brass bed," should actually be "Lie across my big brass bed."

like, such as. Both like and such as may be used in a statement giving an example or a series of examples. Like means similar to; use "like" when comparing the subject mentioned to the examples. *A hurricane, like a flood or any other major disaster, may strain a region's emergency resources.* Use "such as" when the examples represent a general category of things or people. "Such as" is often used as an alternative to for example. *A destructive hurricane, such as Gilbert in 1988, may drastically alter an area's economy.* Commas are not always necessary before and after the phrase containing such as. *Adding fruits such as apples and pears to the bowl should enhance its appearance.* In technical writing, I often use "e.g." instead of such as or for example: *The majority of residents also depend upon fish and game (e.g., trout, salmon, bear, and moose) obtained through subsistence hunting and fishing activities.*

loose, lose. Lose is a verb meaning misplace. Loose, as an adjective, means not securely attached. *Tighten that loose screw before you lose it.*

lots, lots of. Avoid in formal writing.

may be, maybe. May be is a verb phrase. Maybe, the adverb, means perhaps. *She may be the president today, but maybe she will lose the next election.*

media. Media, the plural form of medium, takes a plural verb. The media are going to cover the council meeting.

Ms. Use Ms. instead of Miss or Mrs. unless a woman specifies another title before her name. Ms. should appear before her first name, not before her husband's name: *Ms. Jane Tate*, not Ms. John Tate.

nor, or. Use "either" with "or" and "neither" with "nor."

off of. Use off rather than off of. The spaghetti slipped off the plate.

on, upon. Upon is old-fashioned; usually, "on" is all you need.

only. When you see the word "only" in a sentence, make sure it is in the correct place. The misplacement of the word "only" can completely change a sentence's meaning. *Emily sang only four songs.* (She could have sang many more, but she did not.) *Emily only sang four songs.* (Did Emily just sing a cappella and not play the songs as well? This is confusing.) *Only Emily sang for the guests.* (Perhaps there were numerous other singers, but they did not sing?) *Emily sang four songs only for the invited guests.* (So staff and uninvited guests could not hear her?)

ordnance, ordinance. Ordnance refers to military supplies such as weapons, ammunition, and combat vehicles. Ordinance refers to a decree or order.

owing to the fact that. Avoid this and other unnecessarily word expressions for because.

percent, percentage. These words identify a number as a fraction of 100. Because they show exact statistics, these terms should not be used casually to mean portion, amount, or number. Generally, the word "percent" is always used with a number while "percentage" is not. *Last year, 70 percent of the dogs at animal control were adopted.* In formal writing, spell out percent rather than using its symbol (%) (However, I often use the % symbol in tables.) Percentage is not used with a specific number. *A large percentage of the population prefers fruit to vegetables.*

precede, proceed. Both are verbs; precede means "come before," and proceed means continue or go forward. *Despite the storm that preceded the campus flooding, we proceeded to class.*

principal, principle. These words are unrelated but are often confused because of their similar spellings. Principal as a noun, refers to a head official or an amount of money loaned or invested. When used as an adjective, principal means most significant. The word meaning a fundamental law, belief, or standard is principle. When Albert was sent to the principal, he defended himself with the principle of free speech. The principal intent of the document was to inform.

raise, rise. Raise means lift or move upward. In the case of children, it means bring up or rear. As a transitive verb, it takes a direct object—someone raises something. *The wedding guests raised their glasses in celebration.* Rise means go upwards. It is not followed by a direct object; something rises by itself. *She saw the steam rise from the kettle and knew the tea was ready.*

respectfully, respectively. Respectfully means with respect. Respectively means in the order given. The brothers, respectively a juggler and an acrobat, respectfully greeted the audience.

set, sit. Set means put or place, and it is followed by a direct object—the thing that is placed. Sit does not take a direct object and refers to the action of taking a seat. *Amelia sat at the picnic table and set her backpack on the ground.*

since. Since has two meanings. The first meaning shows the passage of time (*I have not eaten since Tuesday*); the second and more informal meaning is because (*Since you are in a bad mood, I will go away*). Be careful not to write sentences in which since is ambiguous in meaning. *Since I had knee surgery, I have been doing nothing but watching television.* (Since here could mean either because or ever since. In order to avoid such problems some writers prefer not to use since to mean because.)

some body, somebody, some one, someone. *When somebody comes walking down the hall, I always hope that it is someone I know. In dealing with some body like the senate, arrange to meet consistently some one person who can represent the group.*

stationary, stationery. Stationary is an adjective meaning standing still. Stationery is a noun meaning writing paper or materials. *When the bus was stationary at the train crossing, Karen took out her stationery and wrote a letter.*

than, then. Use the conjunction "than" in comparative statements. *The truck was bigger than my house.* Use the adverb "then" when referring to a sequence of events or emotions. *Jim finished college, and then he went to graduate school.*

that, which. That, always followed by a restrictive clause, singles out the object being described. *The trip that you took to New York was expensive.* Note that the clause after "that" is essential to the meaning; it cannot be deleted. Which may be followed by either a restrictive or a nonrestrictive clause but often is used only with the latter. The which clause may simply add more information about a noun or noun clause, and it is set off by commas. *My house, which is in Palmer, is a two-story duplex.* You can delete the phrase in between the commas and still keep the main idea of the sentence that you want to get across. But you cannot delete the words following *that* without losing the meaning of the sentence. *The book that is on the table is the one I want.*

their, there, they're. "Their" is a pronoun, the possessive form of they. *The clients showed their drawings to the editor.* "There" refers to a place. *There, dinosaurs used to walk.* There also is used with the verb "be" in expletive constructions (there is, there are). *There are three items on the agenda.* (I usually try to edit out "there is" and "there are" as they are unnecessary phrases: *The three items on the agenda are dogs, cats, and elephants.*) They're is a contraction of they are, and, like all contractions, it should be avoided in formal writing.

to, too, two. To is a preposition, generally showing direction or nearness. *Stan drove to Eugene.* Avoid using to after where. *Where are you driving?* (not driving to) Too means also. *I am driving there too.* Two is the number.

toward, towards. Towards is considered archaic; toward is now preferred (per Webster's).

visible, visual. Visible means capable of being seen, while visual means pertaining to sight. *No holes were visible in the tank. The method of examination was visual.*

where. Use where alone, not with prepositions such as at or to. *Where did he drill?* (not drill at)

which, who, that. When referring to ideas or things, use which or that. When referring to people, use who or whom. *My aunt, who was furious, pushed on the door, which was still stuck. The book that I like best is* Old Yeller. *The teacher whom I like best is Ms. Pastorelli. People who are interested can sign up after class.*

Interestingly, animals can be referred to by either who or that, depending on the writer's view of them. Sometimes people refer to pets by using the word who and wild animals by using the word that. *Woody, who is my best friend, is a collie. The wolf that ate the rabbits is now in a pen.*

who, whom. Use who if the following clause begins with a verb. *Monica, who drinks uncontrollably, is my godmother. Monica, who is my godmother, drinks uncontrollably.* Use whom in the following clause, which begins with a pronoun. *I have heard that Monica, whom I have not seen for 10 years, wears only purple.* An exception occurs when a verbal phrase such as *I think* comes between who and the following clause. Ignore such a phrase as you decide which form to use. *Monica, who (I think) wears nothing but purple, is my godmother.* Here is a simple way to remember this rule: Can you replace the word with "she"? If so, use who. Can you replace the word with "her" or "them"? If so, use whom. (The phrase "whom I have not seen" becomes "I have not seen her" as you apply this test.)

who's, whose. Who's is the contraction of who and is. Avoid contractions in formal writing. Whose is possessive. *Whose book is on the counter?*

your, you're. Your shows possession. *Bring your pets to the party.* You're is the contraction of you and are. Avoid contractions in formal writing.

12.0 TERMS AND DEFINITIONS

It is a good idea to create a list of commonly used terms and definitions for your company, so that your list can be added to and pulled from for future documents. It is especially important to have a consistent understanding and definition of a term for all personnel.

The following definitions are from various company documents to provide you with an example list. Note that they are in alphabetical order.

One great source for oil company defitnitions is the Schlumberger Oilfield Glossary, which is located here:
http://www.glossary.oilfield.slb.com/

Action Plan

A formal, documented plan that describes the action to be taken, accountable personnel, and required completion date.

Appraisal Plan

The appraisal plan is a formal document that outlines the scope of activities and estimated expenditure in the Appraise and Select stages. The focus of the appraisal plan is to enable an informed decision on project viability and concept selection.

Basis of Design (BOD) Document

The BOD document defines the respective technical basis for the project. It represents conversion of business requirements (given in the statement of requirements) into a technical basis for the project.

Biodiversity

Biodiversity is the variability among living organisms from all sources, including terrestrial, marine, and other aquatic ecosystems, and ecological complexes of which they are part. This includes diversity within species, between species, and of ecosystems. Biodiversity is also about people and our need for food, security, medicines, fresh air and water, shelter, and a clean and healthy environment in which to live.

Brownfield

Site previously and/or currently developed for which development activities have substantially changed the natural character of the site. Brownfields include industrial sites or complexes and other sites with the presence or potential presence of a hazardous substance, pollutant, or contaminant. Brownfields are also characterized by an existing infrastructure that will interface with the project.

Construction Health and Safety Plan

The construction Health and Safety Plan outlines the health and safety organization, policies, and procedures, that are implemented to manage health, safety, and environmental (HSE) risks associated with construction activities.

Constructability Review

A constructability review is a systematic review of the project intended to optimize the use of construction knowledge and experience in planning, engineering, design, fabrication, and installation to achieve overall project and safety objectives.

Environmental Impact Assessment (EIA)/Environmental and Social Impact Assessment (ESIA)

A formal process used to predict environmental and social consequences of the stages of any development project. A process that attempts to identify, predict, and assess the likely consequences of proposed development activities. EIA (or ESIA) ensures that potential problems are foreseen and addressed at an early stage in project planning and design.

Exclusion Zones

A perimeter established for an operating site or project in which nonessential personnel are evacuated during periods of higher risk operation, such as start-ups, shutdowns, and process upsets.

Failure Modes and Effects Analysis (FMEA)

A hazard identification technique in which known failure modes of components or features of a system are considered in turn and undesired outcomes are noted.

Greenfield

Land not previously developed beyond that of agriculture or forestry use. Greenfields are often on the periphery of existing built-up areas or marine areas that have not been subject to offshore oil or gas development. Greenfields are areas that lack infrastructure (e.g., water, power, pipelines, and roads).

Hazard

Condition or practice with the potential to cause harm to people, the environment, property, or the company's reputation.

Hazard and Operability (HAZOP) Analysis

A systematic, qualitative technique to identify and evaluate process hazards and potential operating problems. The methodology uses a series of guidewords to examine deviations from normal process conditions.

Hazard Identification (HAZID) Study

A structured study performed on the process, typically early in design, to identify process hazards. HAZID studies are very broad in scope. The HAZID is sometimes called a preliminary hazard analysis.

Heath Impact Assessment (HIA)

HIA is a combination of procedures, methods, and tools by which a policy, program, or project may be judged as to potential effects on the health of a population and the distribution of those effects within the population.

Health Risk Assessment (HRA)

HRA, in an occupational context, considers the ways in which the work environment and actual tasks to be performed potentially affect the health of workers. HRA may need to cover individual cases or may be generic for a group of people doing the same tasks in the same place. HRA should continue for the life of the project and needs to be appropriate for the degree and complexity of the activities being performed.

Inherently Safer Design (ISD)

The intent of inherently safer design (ISD) is to eliminate the hazard completely or reduce its magnitude sufficiently to eliminate the need for elaborate safety systems and procedures.

Life Cycle Assessment

A technique for assessing plant and hardware from the time of inception through design, construction, operation, and decommissioning.

Lower Tier Subcontractor

A worker who performs actual tasks while under a lengthy contractual chain in which several tiers of subcontractors have been created by repeated subcontracting of the work.

Noncompliance

Not in accordance with our company's standards, practices, or expectations; practices; or regulations.

Nonessential Personnel

Personnel who are not identified by the site or project as essential personnel who need to be on site during higher risk transient operations (i.e., start-ups, shutdowns, upsets, and emergencies) to ensure the safety of the operation.

Premobilization Construction Review

A review conducted prior to a project or contractor mobilizing to the field to commence work. The review examines project and contractor preparedness for construction, including a review of the construction HSE Plan and HSE risks.

Process Hazard Analysis (PHA)

A structured review of the process to identify potential undesired events that could lead to a hazard, and the analysis of the mechanisms by which these undesired events could occur, with the intent of preventing the event or reducing its consequences.

Process Safety

Process safety is a disciplined framework for managing the integrity of hazardous operating systems and processes by applying good design principles, engineering and operating practices. Process safety deals with the prevention and control of incidents that have potential to release hazardous materials or energy. Such incidents can cause toxic effects, fire, or explosion and could ultimately result in serious injuries, property damage, lost production, and environmental impact.

Project HSE Plan

A plan developed by the project team that defines HSE expectations, organizations, and processes to manage HSE risks throughout project development and execution.

Quantified Risk Assessment (QRA)

The systematic engineering/mathematical technique to develop numerical estimates of potential risks based on expected frequency and/or consequence of potential accidents associated with a facility or operation.

Sensitive Areas

Land and sea areas that have been designated or are generally recognized as being of particular biological, geological, topographical, historical, cultural, or spiritual importance or have particularly significant or unique socioeconomic conditions.

Statement of Requirements (SOR)

The SOR describes the fundamental business requirements and success factors for the project and forms the basis upon which project objectives, technical definition, and execution planning are developed.

13.0 ACRONYMS AND ABBREVIATIONS MOST COMMONLY USED AT OUR COMPANY

13.1 Overview

Since this is the first version of our company's style guide, this list of acronyms and abbreviations is a work in progress. Please let the technical editor know of any missing acronyms/abbreviations or of any mistakes in this list. In the meantime, here are some of the acronyms that are currently used in our company's documents, as well as some that might be used in future documents. Again, the most important thing to remember is to be consistent within documents and within the company. Therefore, use this list as a guide for capitalization rules, spelling, and definitions of acronyms. For example, use ArcInfo as presented here instead of ARC/INFO or Arc/Info. *Although all of these forms of ArcInfo have been used in XYZ Company's documents, we have chosen one (based on ESRI's Web site) to use in our documents from now on.*

Note: These are acronyms and abbreviations taken from various company lists and government agency Web site lists; some may not be relevant to your firm, some names may have changed, and your style may be different for others. We suggest that you make notes on your hard copy of which ones to delete, change, or add, as you (or your technical editors) use this document.

If you have purchased our Microsoft Word version of this style guide at our Web site (www.wordsworthwriting.net or www.formsinword.com), you can paste in your own acronym list. We suggest that you paste special, and then select unformatted text, anywhere in the acronym list. Then you can select all the acronyms (the ones here and the new list you have inserted) and choose Table and Sort by paragraph, and you will automatically alphabetize everything. This should save you a lot of time!

Please do let us know (e-mail editor@wordsworthwriting.net) if you see anything that should be changed.

13.2   General Guidelines

General rules for using acronyms and abbreviations follow:

- Always spell out a word or term when it is first used in the text, followed by the acronym or abbreviation in parentheses. You can use the acronym from then on. Examples: The U.S. Environmental Protection Agency (USEPA) and the Alaska Department of Fish and Game (ADF&G) agree that . . .

- It is not necessary to use acronyms. For items appearing only once or twice in a text, it is better to spell them out.

- Standard company style is to include an acronym list at the beginning of each report or proposal. This does not preclude defining each acronym first use, however.

- Please add, delete, and change as you see fit, and turn in your suggestions to the technical editor.

- Certain acronyms and abbreviations are included here that will only be used in figures and tables if needed for spacing, never in the text. Examples include SYST for system.

- Some companies and agencies capitalize all words in their acronyms list, but I do not. I follow the correct capitalization for that term.

13.3   Acronyms & Abbreviations

%	use for "percent" only in table/graph/equation
% Cr	% chromium
$(DE)_j$	dissipated energy in mode number "j"
$(SE)_j$	maximum strain energy in mode number "j"
°C	degrees Celsius
°F	degrees Fahrenheit (*Company* style is 40 °F not 40° F)
1oo1	one out of one
1oo2	one out of two
1oo2D	one-out-of-two diagnostic
24/7	continuous(ly)
2oo2	two out of two
2oo3	two out of three
2oo3D	two-out-of-three diagnostic

3D	three-diameter radius (elbow or bend centerline radius equal to three times the nominal diameter)
3R	three-diameter radius (same as 3D)
4PB	four-point bend
β	yaw (flow inclination) angle between the wind direction to the pipe direction
γ	mode shape participation factor
δ r	reduced damping coefficient
Δx	element length between nodes in finite element model
ε c	longitudinal compressive strain limit corresponding to incipient local buckling
ε p	longitudinal compressive strain limit corresponding to pressure integrity limit state
εs	screening level bending strain
ε t	longitudinal tension strain limit
θ	angle change at horizontal offset distance X: $\theta = \sin^{-1}(X/R_{ins})$
λH	tuning ratio for a high-frequency "H" damper
λL	tuning ratio for a low-frequency "L" damper
λM	tuning ratio for a medium-frequency "M" damper
μg	microgram
μg/kg	microgram per kilogram
μg/L	microgram per liter
μin	microinch
μL	microliter
μm	micrometer
μM or μM	micromolar
μmho	micromho
μmol	micromoles
μS	microsiemen
ν(T)	temperature-dependent kinematic viscosity of air
ξ	damping ratio
ξ n	modal damping ratio for mode number "n"
ρ(T)	temperature-dependent density of air
σ MODAL	modal stress
φdamper-φpipe	relative motion across the damper in the mode shape of interest
φn	mode shape vector for mode number "n"

Ψ	pipe bending curvature, which is equal to the inverse of the bending radius ($\Psi=1/R$)
Ω	ohm

A

Å	angstrom
A or amp	ampere(s)
A&E	alarms and events
A/I&E/E	Automation/Instruments & Controls/Electrical
A/L	artificial lift but use AL instead
A/V	auto variable
A1	acoustical – lead-lined
A2	acoustical – plain
AAC	Alaska Administrative Code
AAEE	American Academy of Environmental Engineers
AAES	American Association of Engineering Societies
AAFE	alternate automatic fire-extinguishing
AAI	ARCO Alaska, Inc. (Note: use ARCO instead of AAI)
AAP	Affirmative Action Plan
AARH	arithmetic average roughness height
AASHTO	American Association of State Highway and Transportation Officials
ABDN	abandoned
ABET	Accreditation Board for Engineering and Technology
ABLC	As-built Location Code
ABMA	American Bearing Manufacturers Association
abs	absolute
ABS	acrylonitrile butadiene styrene
ac	acre
AC	alternating current
AC	armored cable
AC	As Checked
ACC	Anchorage Crisis Center
ACCA	Advisory Committee on Council Activities (standing committee)
ACCP	ASNT Central Certification Program
ACE	advanced collaboration environment
ACEC	American Council of Engineering Companies
acfm	actual cubic foot/feet per minute
ACFM	alternating current field measurement

ac-ft	acre-foot
ACGIH	American Conference of Governmental Industrial Hygienists
ACI	American Concrete Institute
ACM	Association for Computing Machinery
ACM	asbestos-containing material
ACS	Alaska Clean Seas (oil spill cooperative)
ACSM	American Congress on Surveying and Mapping
ACT	American College Testing
ACT	Alaska Consolidated Team
ACT	arctic coiled tubing
ACX	Alpine Capacity Expansion
AD&D	Accidental Death & Dismemberment
ADA	Americans with Disabilities Act
AdCon	Advanced Control
AdCon/O	Advanced Control and Optimization
ADEA	Age Discrimination in Employment Act
ADEC	Alaska Department of Environmental Conservation
ADF&G	Alaska Department of Fish and Game
ADFP	Alaska Division of Fire Prevention
ADHC	Ad Hoc
ADNR	Alaska Department of Natural Resources
ADOL	Alaska Department of Labor
ADPS	Alaska Department of Public Safety
ADR	American Depository Receipts Alternative Dispute Resolution
ADS	American Depository Shares
ADW	Alaska Drilling and Wells
AE	acoustic emission
AEA	Atomic Energy Authority.
AEI	Architectural Engineering Institute
AEP	Annual Engineering Plan
AF	As Fabricated
AF	advanced funding
AFC	Approved for Construction
AFD	authorization for definition
AFE	authorization for expenditure
AFI	Awaiting Further Instructions
AFR	annual facility review

AFT	Anchorage Flight Terminal
AGA	American Gas Association
AGMA	American Gear Manufacturer's Association
AGPF	Aboveground Pipeline Facility
AGT	Azerbaijan-Georgia-Turkey
AHJ	Authority having Jurisdiction
AHRS	Alaska Heritage Resource Survey
AHU	air handling unit
AI	Authorized Inspector
AI	analog input
AI	artificial intelligence
AI	As Installed
AI	Asphalt Institute
AI	Authorized Inspector
AIA	Authorized Inspection Agency
AIA	American Institute of Architects
AIAA	American Institute of Aeronautics and Astronautics
AIC	As Installed Checked
AIChE	American Institute of Chemical Engineers
AIME	American Institute of Mining, Metallurgical and Petroleum Engineers
AIP	Abandoned in Place
AISC	American Institute of Steel Construction
AISI	American Iron and Steel Institute
AIT	auto-ignition temperature
AIV	acoustically induced vibration
AK	Alaska *(U.S. Postal Code; only use in addresses; spell out Alaska in text and tables)*
AK OPS	Alaska Operations
AL	artificial lift (preferred instead of A/L)
ALARP	as low as reasonably practical
ALERT	Asset Leverage Early Risk Team
ALT	Alaska Leadership Team
ALT	Alternate
AM	Area Manager
AMCA	Air Movement and Control Association
AML	Approved Manufacturers List
AMOC	Administrative Management of Change
AMS	Area Maintenance Supervisor

amu	atomic mass unit
AN	audiovisual (equipment)
ANCSA	Alaska Native Claims Settlement Act (P.L. 92-203)
ANS	Alaska North Slope (crude) – use ANSC instead, American Nuclear Society
ANSC	Alaska North Slope Crude Alaska (OSHA)
ANSI	American National Standards Institute
ANWR	Arctic National Wildlife Refuge
AO	analog output
AOB	any other business
AOD	argon oxygen decarbonization
AOGA	Alaska Oil and Gas Association
AOGCC	Alaska Oil and Gas Conservation Commission
AOO	Affects Operation Only
AOPS	Air Operations
AP	Activity Planning
AP	Administrative Policy *(from NCEES Manual of Policy and Position Statements)*
APB	acid-producing bacteria
APB	annular pressure buildup
APC	Alaska Petroleum Contractors
APC	Asset Production Chemist
APE	Area Petroleum Engineer
APEC	Asia-Pacific Economic Cooperation
APE'S	Area Petroleum Engineers (in Anchorage)
APF	Alpine Processing Facility
API	American Petroleum Institute
API RP	American Petroleum Institute Recommended Practice
APL	Approved Suppliers List
APOC	Alaska Public Offices Commission
APR	Asset Performance Review
APSC	Alyeska Pipeline Service Company *(Sometimes APS is used; replace with this.)*
APU	Alaska Pacific University
Ar	argon
ARCO	Atlantic Richfield Co.
ARE	Architect Registration Examination
AREMA	American Railway Engineering and Maintenance of Way Association

ARM	Alarm Response Manual
ARPA	advanced radar plotting aid
ARV	atmospheric relief valve
AS	Alaska Statute
ASAC	Applied Science Accreditation Commission
ASAE	American Society of Agricultural Engineers
ASB	asbestos
ASBOG	Association of State Boards of Geology
ASBT	As-Built
ASCCP	Asset Specific Corrosion Control Plan
ASCE	American Society of Civil Engineers
ASCG	Arctic Slope Consulting Group
ASCI	Alaska Supply Chain Integrators
ASD	Allowable Stress Design; or Adjustable Speed Drive
ASEE	American Society for Engineering Education
ASH	Alaska Safety Handbook
ASHRAE	American Society of Heating, Refrigerating, and Air-Conditioning Engineers
AS-i	actuator sensor interface
ASL	Approved Suppliers List
ASM	Abnormal Situation Management
ASM	Abnormal Situation Management® Consortium
ASME	American Society of Mechanical Engineers (seems to go by ASME only now; see asme.org)
ASNT	American Society for Nondestructive Testing
ASPRS	American Society for Photogrammetry and Remote Sensing
ASQ	American Society for Quality
ASS	austenitic stainless steel
AST	aboveground storage tank
ASTM	ASTM International *(formerly American Society for Testing and Materials)*
ASV	annular safety valve
at wt	atomic weight
ATC	Actuator Technology Company *(trademark)*
ATEX	Explosive Atmospheres *(European Union standard)*
atm	atmosphere
ATP	advanced technology parts
ATP	Authorization to Proceed

ATRT	automated tangential radiographic technique
ATS	automatic transfer switch
ATV	all-terrain vehicle
AUT	automatic ultrasonic testing
AUV	autonomous underwater vehicle
Avg/min	average/minimum
AVL	Approved Vendors List
AVR	automatic voltage regulator
AVT	ad valorem tax
AWG	American Wire Gauge
AWOS	Automated Weather Observation System
AWPA	American Wood Preserver's Association
AWS	American Welding Society
AWWA	American Water Works Association

B

B	Bend angle in degrees
B	billion
B	inherent control valve pressure drop (PD) allowance
B	boron
B&PV	Boiler and Pressure Vessel
BAD	Badami
bar(a)	bar(s) absolute
bar(g)	bar(s) gauge
bara	bar(s) absolute – *use bar(a)*
barg	bar(s) gauge – *use bar(g)*
BB	bolted bonnet
BBE	beveled both ends
bbl	barrel (42 gallons)
bbls	barrels
BBS	behavior-based safety
BC	bolt circle
bd ft	board foot
BDV	blowdown valve
BE	beveled end
BEP	best efficiency point
BER	business expense report
BESD	blowdown emergency shutdown
BF	base flange

BF	blind flange
BFE	base flange elevation
BG	bell guide
bgs	below ground surface
BHA	bottom hole assembly
BHCS	borehole compensated sonic log
BHL	bottom hole location
BHN	Brinnel Hardness
BHP	bottom hole pressure
BHP	brake (horse) power
BHT	bottom hole temperature
Binherent	control valve pressure drop (PD) allowance
BL	balance line
BLD	block layout drawing
BLE	beveled large end
BLE/PSE	beveled large end/plain small end
BLE/TSE	beveled large end/threaded small end
BLEVE	boiling liquid expanding vapor explosion
BLM	braided line measurement
BLM	Bureau of Land Management
BLMD	braided line measured depth
BLS	Bureau of Labor Statistics
BOC	Base Operations Center or Base Oil Camp or Base Operation Camp
BOCA	Building Officials and Code Administrators International
BoD	Basis of Design; note, not BOD
BOD/BoD	Board of Directors (NCEES usage)
BOEPD	barrels of oil equivalent per day
BOF	basic oxygen furnace
BOL	bottom of line
BOM	Bill of Materials
BOM	bill/balance of material
BOMA	ball-out mud acid job
BOP	balance of project
BOP	blowout preventer
bopd	barrels of oil per day
bp	boiling point
BP	bridge plug

BPCS	basic process control system
bpd	barrels per day
BPS	bulk power supply
BPV	back pressure valve
BPVC	Boiler Pressure Vessel Code
BPXA	BP Exploration (Alaska) Inc.
BRC	basic regulatory control
BS	back side or base sediments
BS	British Standard
BS&W	basic sediment and water
bscfd	billion standard cubic feet per day
BSE	beveled small end
BSI	British Standards Institute
BSTG	Buncefield Standards Task Group
BTC	Baku-Tbilisi-Ceyhan
Btu	British thermal unit
$Btu/hr/ft^2$	British thermal units per hour per square foot
BU	Business Unit
BUL	Business Unit Leader
BV	ball valve (SSSV)
BVN	ball valve nipple (SSSV nipple)
BW	butt-weld
BWG	British Wire Gauge
bwpd	barrels of water per day
BWRS	Benedict-Webb-Rubin-Starling

C

C	carbon
C	material constant used to define fatigue characteristics
C&E	cause and effect
C&I	Control and Instrumentation
C&M	Corrosion and Materials
C/S	Civil/Structural
C/S	client/server
C'L	fluctuating lift coefficient
C_2H_6	ethane (hydrocarbon gas)
C^2Ed	Center for Collaboration and Education in Design
CA	Certifying Authority
CA	Compliance Authority

CA	corrosion allowance
CAA	Clean Air Act
CaClO$_2$	calcium hypochlorite
CAD	computer-aided design
CAE	cost of additional equipment
CAF	compressed asbestos fiber
CAM	Contract Accountable Manager
CAN	controller area network
CAO	Corrective Action Order (U.S. Department of Transportation)
CAOP	calculated allowable operating pressure
CAP SUST	capacity sustainment
CAP	capacity
CAP	Capital Accumulation Plan
CAPEX	capital expenditures
CARB	carbolite
CART	Cartridge
CAS	Canadian Standards Association
CASE	Council of American Structural Engineers of ACEC
CASS	Conformity Assessment of Safety-related Systems
CBA	cost benefit analysis
CBS	cost breakdown structure
CBT	computer-based training
CBT	cement bond tool
CBT	computer-based testing
CC	Construction Camp
CC	control center
CCA	critical corrective action
CCD	charge coupled device (digital video)
CCL	casing collar locator
CCP	Corrosion Control Program
CCP	Central Compression Plant
CCPE	Canadian Council of Professional Engineers
CCPS	Center for Chemical Process Safety
CCR	centralized control room
CCS	communication control system
CCS	Corrosion Control Strategy
CCSM	Corrosion Control Strategy Manager
CCTV	closed-circuit television

CD	compact disk
CD	compact drill site
CDB	common database
CDM	Construction Design and Management
CDN	Colville Drill Site, North, Also known as Fiord
CDO	certified dimension outlines
CDRL	contractor's document requirements listing
CD-ROM	compact disk read-only memory
CDS	Colville Drill Site, South, Also known as Nanuq
CDS	Conceptual Design Study
CE	carbon equivalent
CE	Construction Engineer
CE	Corrosion Engineer
CEAB	Canadian Engineering Accreditation Board
CE_{IIW}	carbon equivalent (IIW formula)
CELSOC	Consulting Engineers and Land Surveyors of California
CEM	Corrosion Engineers Meeting (weekly)
CEMS	Corrosion Erosion Management System
CEN	European Committee for Standardization
CEO	Chief Executive Officer
CERCLA	Comprehensive Environmental Response, Compensation, and Liability Act (Superfund)
CESB	Council of Engineering Specialty Boards
CET	Cement Evaluation Tool
cf/h	cubic foot/feet per hour
CFC	chlorofluorocarbons
cfd or ft^3/day	cubic foot/feet per day
CFD	computerized fluid dynamics
CFF	common file format
cfm or ft^3/min	cubic foot/feet per minute
CFP	Central Facility Plant
CFR	Code of Federal Regulations
CFR	critical flow rate
cfs or ft^3/sec	cubic foot/feet per second
C_g	valve sizing coefficient for gas
CGF	Central Gas Facility
CGR	condensate gas ratio
CH_3COOH	acetic acid
CH_4	methane

CHAZOP	Computer Hazard and Operability (study)
CHIP	Chemical Hazards Information and Packaging
CHK	choke
CHKS	back flow checks
CHOPS	Cold Heavy Oil Production with Sand
CI	Continuous Improvement
CI	corrosion inhibitor (*also defined as corrosion inhibition; inhibitor seems to be preferred*)
CIA	Chemical Industries Association
CIBP	cast iron bridge plug
CICIND	International Committee on Industrial Chimneys
CID	Corrosion Inhibitor Development Process
CIL	commercial integrity level
CIL	corrosion inspection location
CIP	Comprehensive Inspection Plan
CIPS	Close Interval Potential Survey
CISCC	chloride stress corrosion cracking
CIT	corrosion inhibitor treatment
CL	Class
CL	control line/carbolite
CLARB	Council of Landscape Architectural Registration Boards
CLEAR	Council on Licensure, Enforcement, and Regulation
ClGNA	Connecticut General Life Insurance Company
CLR	crack length ratio
CLSA	California Land Surveyors Association
CLV	Cleveland
cm	centimeter(s)
CM	Crisis Manager
cm/sec	centimeter(s) per second
cm^2	square centimeter
cm^3	cubic centimeter (cc for gas volume only)
cm^3-sec	cubic centimeter-second
CMAS	Competency Management Assurance System
CMI	control, monitoring and inspection
CML	corrosion monitoring location
CMMS	Computerized Maintenance Management System
C-Mn	carbon-manganese
CMP	corrugated metal pipe
CMS	Chemical Managed Services

CMT	cement
CMT	Crisis Management Team
CMTR	Certified Material Test Report
CMU	Crisis Management Unit
CN	control narrative
CND	condensate
CNL	compensated neutron log
CNST	construction
CNW	commercially navigable waterway
CO	carbon monoxide
CO	controller output
CO_2	carbon dioxide
COBRA	Consolidated Omnibus Budget Reconciliation Act of 1985
COD	cash on delivery
COE	Corps of Engineers *(do not use; replaced with USACE)*
CoL	Competency on Line
COM	component object model (Microsoft)
Conc	Concentric
CONCAWE	Conservation of Clean Air and Water – Europe
CONSOP	control safety and operability
CONV. PORT	Conventional Port
CoP	Community of Practice
COP	Current Operational Period
COPA	Council on Post Secondary Accreditation
COSHH	Control of Substances Hazardous to Health
COTS	commercial, off-the-shelf
COTU	Crude Oil Topping Unit
CoW	Control of Work
COWPS	Council on Wage and Price Stability
CP	cathodic protection
cP	centipoise
CP	control philosophy
CPA	Certified Professional Accountant
CPAI	ConocoPhillips Alaska, Inc.
CPC	continuing professional competency
CPD	continuing professional development
CPF	Central Production Facility
CPI	continuous performance improvement

C-plan	contingency plan
cpm	cycles per minute
CPR	cardiopulmonary resuscitation
cps or Hz	cycles per second
CPS	Central Power Station
CPS	Certified Professional Secretary
CPT	critical pitting temperature
CPU	Central Processing Unit
CPVC	chlorinated polyvinyl chloride
CQPM	Construction Quality Program Manual
Cr 13	chrome tubing *(also defined as 13 chromium or 13 chrome; 13% Cr (chrome) seems to be preferred at some companies)*
Cr	chromium
CR	polychloroprene (chloroprene rubber) (e.g., Neoprene®)
CR	Concession Request
CR	control room
CR	corrosion rate
CR	Criticality Rating
CRA	corrosion-resistant alloy
CRI	cuttings reinjection
CRM	corrosion-resistant material
CRM	corrosion rate monitoring
Cr-Ni	chromium-nickel
CRR	continuous risk reduction
CRT	computerized radiographic technique
CRT	cathode ray tube
CRT	Control Room Technician (board operator)
CRT	Crisis Response Team
CS	carbon steel
CS	catcher sub or circulating sub
CS	control suite
CSA	Canadian Standards Association (Canada)
CSC	car seal (or sealed) closed
CSC	Computer Support Center
CSC/CSO	car seal(ed) closed/car seal(ed) open (normally applies to isolation valves)
CSCC	chloride stress corrosion cracking
CSD	control strategy diagram

CSE	Concept Safety Evaluation
CSH	control system hardware
CSI	Construction Specifications Institute
CSO	car seal(ed) open
CSP	cold storage pad
CSP	Corrosion Strategy and Planning
CSP	corrugated steel pipe
CSR	crack sensitivity ratio
CST	cost of spurious trips per year
CSTF	Central Sewage Treatment Facility
CSWIP	Certification Scheme for Welding and Inspection Personnel
CT	coiled tubing
CT	current transformer
CTD	cumulative trauma disorder
CTG	Computer Task Group
CTI	Cooling Technology Institute
CTL	Corrosion Team Lead
CTM	Compliance Task Manager
CTN	coiled tubing nozzle
CTOD	crack tip opening displacement (test)
CTR	crack thickness ratio
CTRNG	centering
CTRT	C-Arm tangential radiographic technique
CTU	coiled tubing unit
CTUWO	coiled tubing unit workover
Cu	copper
CUF	corrosion under fireproofing
CUI	corrosion under insulation
Cu-Ni	copper-nickel
Cv	coefficient of flow
CV	control valve
Cv	control valve sizing coefficient
CV	controlled variable
CVD	chemical vapor deposition
CVN	Charpy V-Notch (impact test)
CVP	Capital Value Process
CWA	Clean Water Act
CWC	Cold Weather Contractor

CWE	Certified Welding Educator
CWEng	Certified Welding Engineer
CWI	Certified Welding Inspector
CWR	control work release
CWTF	Central Water Treatment Facility
cy	cubic yard

D

D	daily
D	diagnostics (in a voting group option)
D	diameter
D	flame detector effective viewing distance
D	insulated diameter of pipeline
D	uninsulated pipe outside diameter
D&C	Drilling and Completion
D&ID	ducting and instrumentation diagram
D/A	digital to analog
D/t	diameter divided by wall thickness
D2D	data to desktop
DA	data access
DA	Direct Assessment
DAE	design accidental event
DAFWC	Day Away from Work Case
DAS	Data Sheet
Dav	detection distance (average)
DAW	Data Analysis Workbook
DB	database
dB	decibel(s)
DB	dump bailer
dB/m	decibels per meter
dBA	decibel(s), A-weighted
DBB	double block and bleed
DBHE	diffusion-bonded heat exchanger
DBMS	database management system
DBV	dummy ball valve
DC	direct current
DCA	decline curve analysis
DCGV	direct current ground voltage – measurement of cathodic protection current leakage to ground

DCMS	Document Control Management System
DCOM	Distributed Component Object Model
DCR	design change request
DCS	Distributed Control System
DCT	Digital & Communications Technology
DCVG	direct current voltage gradient
DD	device description
DD&A	depreciation, depletion, and amortization
DD&R	Decomissioning, Dismantlement and Restoration
DDB	drive-down bailer
DDE	dynamic data exchange
DDL	device description language
DDR	Design Deviation Request
DE	drive end
DEA	diethanolamine
DEM	Design Engineering Manual
DEMO	demolition
DES	Design Engineering Supervisor
DFP	Division of Fire Prevention
DFT	dry film thickness
DG	dummy (perforating) gun
DGC	Department of Governmental Coordination
DGF	dispersed gas flotation (cell)
DGLV	dummy gas lift valve
DGN	MicroStation File Extension
DGPS	Differential Global Positioning System
DH	down hole
DHS	Data Historian System
DHSV	downhole safety valve
DHT	dehydrogenation heat treatment
DI	damaged insulation
DI	discrete input
DIC	Deputy Incident Commander
DIL	dual induction log
DIN	Deutsches Institut für Normung
DIOM	Design, Installation, Operation, and Maintenance (manual)
DIPA	diisopropanolamine
DIPR-1	Design in Progress Review 1,2 etc.

DIS	Draft International Standard
DISC	disconnect
DKW	drinking water supply
DL	dead leg
DLB	ductile-level blast
DLE	ductile-level event
DLIR	Dead Leg Identification Register
DLL	data link layer
DLL	dual laterolog
DLR	Dead Leg Register
DMD	driller's measured depth
DMS	document management system
DN	nominal diameter
DNR	Department of Natural Resources
DNV	Det Norske Veritas
DO	discrete output
DO	dissolved oxygen
DOA	dead on arrival
DOC	document
DOC	Deputy On-Scene Commander
DOE	U.S. Department of Energy
DOF	degree of freedom
DOL	United States Department of Labor
DOP	Departmental Operating Procedure
DOR	Department of Revenue
DOSC	Deputy Operations Section Chief
DOT	U.S. Department of Transportation
DP	differential pressure (pressure drop)
dp	differential pressure across the valve
DP	dynamic positioning
DPB	dollars per barrel
DPDT	double pole, double throw
DPI	dots per inch
DPI	dye-penetrant inspection
DPS	double-piston seat
DPT	Drilling Planning Team
DPV	depressuring valve
DR	Deviation Request
DR	digital radiography

DRA	drag-reducing agent
DRE	destruction removal efficiency
DRLG	drilling
DRT	digital radiographic testing
DS 1J	Drill Site 1J
DS	Dowell-Schlumberger or Drill Site
DS	downstream
DS	drill site (cap if used with a specific drill site, as in Drill Site 1J)
DS/WP	Drill Site and/or Well Pad (the same types of facilities are called drill sites in the EOA, and well pads in the WOA)
DSAW	double submerged arc-welded (pipe) (API terminology but synonymous with SAW)
DSB	downstream benefits
DSC	Distributive Control System
DSD	Defeated Safety Device
DSGN	Design
DSI	Document Storage, Inc.
DSL	diesel
DSP	Decision Support Package
DSS	duplex stainless steel
DST	Drill Stem Test
DSX	drill site expansion
DTL	Design Team Lead
DTS	Daily Time Sheet
DV	dependent variable
DW	Drinking Water Unusually Sensitive Area
DWD	dirty water disposal
DWDI	double wall double image
DWG	drawing (AutoCAD File Extension)
DWO	Drilling and Well Operations
DWS	Daily Work Schedule
DWSI	double wall single image
DWT	dirty water tank
DWTT	drop weight tear test
DX	data exchange (refer also to OPC DX)

E

e	error

E	pipe modulus of elasticity
E&P MPcp	Upstream Segment Major Projects common process
E/E/PE	electrical/electronic/programmable electronic *(use instead of E/E/P)*
EA	Engineering Authority
EA	Environmental Assessment
EAC	Engineering Accreditation Commission
EAP	Employee Assistance Program
EAQ	Education Assessment and Qualification (standing committee)
EATF	Environmental Affairs Task Force
EBI	external bus interface
EC	erosion-corrosion
EC	engineering contract
ECA	Engineering Critical Assessment
ECB	electrical circuit breaker
ECC	Eccentric (line class docs)
ECC	Engineering College Council
ECDA	External Corrosion Direct Assessment
ECEI	Engineering Credentials Evaluation International
ECN	engineering change notice
ECO	Ecological Unusually Sensitive Area
ECPM	Engineering Contract Project Manager
EDDI	Engineering Drawing and Document Information
EDDRP	Engineering Drawing/Document Requirements Procedure Guidelines
EDM	exciter diode monitor
EDP	emergency depressuring
EDP	emergency depressurization
EDPV	emergency depressuring valve
EDS	energy dispersive spectroscopy
EDTA	ethylene diamine tetra acetic (acid)
EEA	European Economic Area
EEA	European Environment Agency
EEMUA	Engineering Equipment and Materials Users Association
EEO	Equal Employment Opportunity
EEOC	Equal Employment Opportunity Commission
EER	Escape, Evacuation, and Rescue (study)
EFAT	Extended Factory Acceptance Test

EFC	European Federation of Corrosion
EFM	electrical field mapping (corrosion monitoring technique, also known as FSM).
EFW	electric fusion welded/welding
EG	ethylene glycol
EHA	Explosion Hazard Analysis
EI	Electrical and Instrumentation
EI	Energy Institute
EI	Engineer Intern
EIA	Electronic Industries Association
EIA	Environmental Impact Assessment
EIA	Equipment Integrity Assurance
EIAGs	Equipment Integrity Assurance Guidelines
EIL	environmental integrity level
EIMP	Environmental Impact Management Process
EIS	Environmental Impact Statement
EIT	Engineer-in-Training
EIW	electric induction welding/welded
EJMA	Expansion Joint Manufacturers Association
ELMD	electric line measured depth
ELQ	emergency living quarters
ELQTF	Engineering Licensure Qualifications Task Force (ad hoc committee)
ELSES	Engineering and Land Surveying Examination Services
EM	expanded metal personnel protection
EMAT	electromagnetic acoustic transducer
EMC	electromagnetic compatibility
emf	electromagnetic force
EMF	electromotive force (voltage)
EMFL	External Magnetic Flux Leakage
EMI	electromagnetic examination
EMI	electromagnetic interference
EmOC	Emergency Operations Center
EMP	electromagnetic pulse
EMP	Equipment Maintenance Planning Team – under M&R
EMR	Engineering Material Request
EMR	Engineering Material Requisition
EMS	Emergency Medical Services
EMS	Environmental Management System

EMT	electrical metallic tubing
EMT	Emergency Medical Technician
emu	electromagnetic unit
EN	electrochemical noise
EN	European Standard
END	Endicott
ENP	electroless nickel plating
ENVID	Environmental Identification
EOA	Eastern Operating Area
EOB	explanation of benefits
EOC	Eastern Operating Center (ARCO's Production Control)
EOC	Eastern Operations Control (Center)
EOL	elbolet
EOR	Enhanced Oil Recovery
EOS	equation of state
EOT	end of tubing
EOT	enhanced organizational team
EOV	effectively owned vessels
EP	Equalizing Prong
EP	examination policy *(from the NCEES Manual of Policy and Position Statements)*
EPA	U.S. Environmental Protection Agency *(some companies prefer USEPA)*
EPC	Engineering, Procurement, and Construction
EPCRA	Emergency Planning and Community Right to Know Act
EPD	emergency depressuring
EPD	equipment protection device
EPDM	ethylene-propylene-diene-monomer
EPE	Examinations for Professional Engineers (standing committee)
EPMS	Engineering and Project Management Services
EPP	Examination Policy and Procedures (standing committee)
EPR	Environmental Performance Requirement
EPRG	European Pipeline Research Group
EPROM	electrically programmable read-only memory
EPS	expanded polystyrene
EPS	Examinations for Professional Surveyors (standing

	committee)
EPT	Engineering Project Tracking
EPT	Exploration and Production Technology
EPWZ	Eastern Peripheral Wedge Zone
EQP	Eagle Quantum Premier
EQUIP	equipment
ER	electric resistance (probes)
ERA	Environmental Risk Assessment
ERC	Emergency Response Coordinator
ERF	engineering repair factor
ERF	estimated repair factor
ERISA	Employee Retirement Income Security Act (1974)
ERM	erosion rate monitoring
ERNP	Environmental Requirements for New Projects
ERP	Enterprise Resource Planning
ERP	Environmental Performance Requirements
ERPG	Emergency Response Planning Guideline
ERPG-2	Emergency Response Planning Guideline Level 2, U.S. National Oceanic and Atmospheric Administration
ERT	Emergency Response Team (fire)
ERV	Escort Response Vessel
ERW	electric resistance welded/welding
ES	equalizing sleeve
ESD	emergency shutdown
ESDV	emergency shutdown valve
ESIA	Environmental and Social Impact Assessment
ESIB	Expense Shared Investment Basis
ESOP	Employee Stock-Ownership Plan
ESOS	Executive Share Option Scheme
ESP	electrical submersible pump
ESRI	Environmental Systems Research Institute
ESS	Emergency Support System
ESS	emergency support system
ESW	electroslag welding
et al.	et alia (and others) *don't define but always use with ( ) and comma as in (e.g., xxx)*
ET	electric heat-traced insulation service
ETA	estimated time of arrival
etc.	et cetera don't define; generally we try to avoid in

	technical writing if we can
ETP	Engineering Technical Practice
eV	electron volt
EW	effluent water
EWE	Eileen West End
EWI	Edison Welding Institute
EWS	emergency warning system
EWT	early well tie-in
Ex d	flameproof electrical fitting specification
Ext PoF	External Probability of Failure

F

F	fire protection
F&E	fire and explosion
F&G	fire and gas
F/N	frequency (of hazard)/number (of fatalities)
FABSITE	Fabrication Site
FAC	field action request
FAC	flow-assisted corrosion
FACP	fire alarm control panel
FAD	failure assessment diagram
FAI	Fauske & Associates, Inc.
FAT	Factory Acceptance Test(ing)
FB	full bore
FB	function block
FBE	fusion-bonded epoxy
FBI	Federal Bureau of Investigation
FBR	full-bore rupture
FBW	flash butt-welding
FC	field crew
FCAW	flux cored arc welding
FCC	Federal Communications Commission
FCC	fluid catalytic cracking
FCCU	fluid catalytic cracking unit
FCI	Fluid Controls Institute, Inc.
FCO	functionality checkout
FCR	field change request
FCR	Field Concession Request
FCV	flow control valve

FDC	formation density log
FDL	flash drum liquids
FDP	Field Development Plan
FDS	functional design specification
F-E	cumulative frequency (F) against environmental impact (E)
FE	Fundamentals of Engineering exam or Field Engineer
Fe	iron
FE-13	DuPont trade name for HFC-23, a Halon substitute
FEA	finite element analysis
$FeCl_3$	ferric chloride
FEED	front-end engineering design
FEHA	Fire and Explosion Hazard Analysis
FEHM	Fire and Explosion Hazard Management
FEHMP	Fire and Explosion Hazard Management Plan
FEHR	Fire and Explosion Hazard Register
FEL	front-end loading
FEL-2	front-end loading (Conceptual Design)
FEL-3	front-end loading (Preliminary Engineering)
FEP	fluorinate, ethylene, propylene
FES	fire and explosion strategy
FeS	iron sulfide
FF	flat (or full) face
FF	FOUNDATION™ Fieldbus
f_{ff}	frequency corresponding to fixed-fixed boundary conditions within a single span
FFG	flame front generator
FFGU	field fuel gas unit
FFKM	perfluoroelastomer
FFM	full field model
FFP	fitness for purpose (or, if adjective preceding noun: fitness-for purpose)
FFS	fitness for service (or, if adjective preceding noun: fitness-for-service) (I guess spell out fit for service)
FFSA	fitness for service assessment
FGACP	fire and gas alarm control panel
f_H	frequency of a high frequency "H" damper
FHA	Fire Hazard Analysis
FI	Film/Data Interpreter

FICA	Federal Insurance Contributions Act
FIG	International Federation of Surveyors
FIMS	Facilities Integrity Management System
FIMS	Facility Integrity Management System
FIP	Frequent Inspection Program
FISCO	Fieldbus Intrinsically Safe Concept
FIT	frac isolation tool (covers BVN)
FIV	flow induced vibration
FKM	fluoroelastomer
FL	flow line
FL	fluid loss
f_L	frequency of a low frequency "L" damper
FLACS	Flame Acceleration Simulator
FLG	flanged
Flgd.	flanged
FLIR	forward-looking infrared
FLS	Fundamentals of Land Surveying exam
FLSA	Fair Labor Standards Act
FM	Fire Marshall
FM	Factory Mutual Research (U.S., Canada)
FM	Financial Memorandum
FM	FM Global Technologies LLC (also known as FM Approvals and formerly Factory Mutual Research Corporation)
FM	Fracmaster
f_M	frequency of a medium frequency "M" damper
FME	Field Mechanical Engineer
FMEA	Failure Mode and Effects Analysis
FMECA	Failure Modes, Effects, and Criticality Analysis
FMLA	Family and Medical Leave Act
FMRC	Factory Mutual Research Corporation [SEE FM; NAME CHANGED]
FMS	wind/wave measure (fast-magneto-sonic)
FMS	Fieldbus messaging specification
FMT	Field Management Team
FMX	flowline and manifold expansion
F-N	cumulative frequency (F) against number of fatalities (N)

FN	ferrite number (per Welding Research Council Bulletin Number 342)
FN	fishing neck
fn	frequency for mode number "n"
FNICO	Fieldbus Nonincendive Concept
FO	fiber optic
FOC	fiber-optic cable
FOD	foreign object debris
FOI	Freedom of Information (federal Act)
FOM	Field Operations Manager
FOSC	Federal On-Scene Coordinator
FOV	field of view
FP	Financial Policy (from the NCEES Manual of Policy and Position Statements)
FP	fluid-packed
FPB	four-point bend.
FPD	freezing point depression
FPE	fire protective equipment
fpm or ft/min	foot/feet per minute
fpp	frequency corresponding to pinned-pinned boundary conditions within a single span
FPQ	Foaming Procedure Qualification
FPRG	Facility Planning Review Group
fps or ft/sec	foot/feet per second
FPSO	floating production, storage, and offloading (facility; or unit)
FRA	Fire Risk Analysis
FRAC	formation fracture operation
FRC	fire-resistant clothing
FRI	Fractionation Research Incorporated
FRP	fiber-reinforced plastic
FS	flow station or Facility Superintendent (cap flow station if used with a number, as in Flow Station 1 [FS1])
FS	forged steel
FS	functional specification
fs	vortex shedding frequency
FSA	Functional Safety Assessment
FSC	Finance Section Chief
FSD	fire and gas shutdown

FSS	fluid-sampling system
ft	foot or feet (spell out in text; only use in tables and figures if needed)
ft/s	foot/feet per second
ft/sec	foot/feet per second
ft^2	square foot/feet
ft^2h	square feet per hour
ft^3	cubic foot/feet
ft^3/lb	cubic feet per pound
FTA	flow line termination assembly
FTE	full-time equivalent
ft-lb	foot-pound
ft-lbs.	foot-pounds
FTP	Flowing Tubing Pressure
FUTA	Federal Unemployment Tax Act
FV	flapper valve (SSSV)
FW	firewater
fw	wake frequency
FWHP	Flowing Wellhead Pressure
FWM	fine water mist (spray system)
Fy	specified minimum yield stress
FYI	for your information
FYP	5-year plan

G

g	acceleration due to gravity
g	gram
G	gravitational constant
g/cc	grams per cubic centimeter
g/cm^2	grams per square centimeter
g/l	grams per liter
g/m^2	grams per square meter
g/m^3	grams per cubic meter
GA	general arrangement drawing
GA	Global Agreement
ga.	gauge
gal	gallon
gal/day	gallons per day
GAnB	general anaerobic bacteria

GBA	General Bridge Act
GC	Gathering Center
GCC	gas cap cycling
GCI	gas cap injection
GCL	geosynthetic clay liner
$g\text{-}cm^2$	gram-square centimeter
GCT	gyro continuous tool
GD	gravity drainage
GDP	Group Defined Practice
GDWFI	gravity drainage waterflood interaction
GFCI	ground fault circuit interrupter
GHB	general heterotrophic bacteria
GHG	greenhouse gas
GHSC	galvanically induced hydrogen stress cracking
gHSEr	getting Health, Safety, and Environment right
gHSSEr	getting Health, Safety, Security, and Environment right
GHX	gas handling expansion
GHX-2	gas handling expansion - (Phase) 2
GHz	gigahertz
GI	gas injection
GIAAPS	Group Investment Assurance and Approval Processes
GIF	Graphic Interchange Format
GIS	Group Instruction for Supply
GIS	Geographic Information System
GJ	ground joint
GL	gas lift
GLM	gas lift mandrel
GLOC	gross light oil column
GLPA	Global Line Pipe Agreement
GLT	gas lift (WOA heritage)
GLT	gas lift transit
GLT	lift gas for wells
GLTI	gas lift tubing inhibition
GLV	gas lift valve
GM	General Manager
GMAW	gas metal arc welding
GMS	Generic Maintenance Strategy
GO	gear-operated
GOC	gas oil contact

GOFR	general-purpose optical fiber raceway
GoM	Gulf of Mexico
GOP	Gross Over-moment Protection
GOR	gas oil ratio
GOR	gas-to-oil ratio
GORC	Group Operations Risk committee
GP	poorly graded gravel (USCS Group Symbol)
Gp	Process gain
GPA	Global Pipeline Agreement
gpad	gallons per acre per day
GPB	Greater Prudhoe Bay
gpd	gallon(s) per day
gpf	gallons per flush
gpm	gallons per minute
GPMA	Greater Point McIntyre Area
GPO	General Projects Organization
GPS	Global Positioning System
gps	gallons per second
GPT	Global Procurement Team
GPU	gas-driven pump unit
gr	grain
Gr	Grade (not GR)
Grafoil	Graphite Foil
GRE	glass-fiber-reinforced epoxy
GRG	Gas Reserves Group or Gas Redetermination Group
GRP	glass-reinforced piping
GRP	glass-reinforced plastic or glass-fiber-reinforced plastics
GSC	wet gas conditioning
GS-FCAW	gas-shielded flux-cored arc welding
GSO	gas shut off
GT	glycol heat-traced insulation service
GTAW	gas tungsten arc welding
GTG	Gas Turbine Generator
GTL	gas to liquids
GUI	graphical user interface
GUL	Group Universal Life Plan
GUL	Guided Ultrasonics Ltd.
GW	guideword
GW	girth weld

GW	groundwater
GW	well-graded gravel, fine to coarse gravel (USCS Group Symbol)
GWUT	guided wave ultrasonic testing

H

H	identifier for a "high" frequency damper for primary modes
H	static head (head difference between entrance and exit)
H&V	heating and ventilation
H:V	horizontal to vertical
H1	H1 is a term used to describe a fieldbus network operating at 31.25 kbit/second.
H_2	hydrogen
H_2CO_3	carbonic acid
H_2O	water
H_2S	hydrogen sulfide (NOT sulphide; that's British spelling)
H_2SO_4	sulfuric acid
HALCO	Halliburton Service Company
HAP	hazardous air pollutant
HAZ	heat-affected zone
HAZAN	hazard analysis
HAZCOM	Hazard Communications
HAZCON	hazards of construction
HAZID	hazard identification (study)
HAZMAT	hazardous materials
HAZOP	Hazard and Operability (study)
HAZWOPER	Hazardous Waste Operations and Emergency Response (OSHA 1910.120)
HB	Brinell hardness
HB	hardness – Rockwell B Scale
HBW	Brinell hardness measured by tungsten carbide ball (also referred to as HB)
HCA	High Consequence Area
HCl	hydrogen chloride
HCL	hydrochloride
HCN	hydrogen cyanide
HCP	Handover Certification Pack
HCRA	Health Care Reimbursement Account
HCU	hydro cracking unit

HDD	horizontal directional drill/drilling
HDPE	high-density polyethylene
HDS	hydrodesulfurization
HEI	Heat Exchange Institute
HEM	Homogenous Equilibrium Model
HF	high frequency
HF	hydrofluoric acid
HF	hydrogen fluoride
HFA	Human Factors Analysis
HFA	*note HFA is not hydroflouric acid; use HF instead*
HFC	hydrofluorocarbon
HF-ERW	high-frequency electric-resistance welded
HFI	high-frequency induction
HFL	higher flammability limit
HFW	high-frequency welded
HHC	highly hazardous chemical
HHL	high-high liquid
HI YLD	high yield
HIA	Health Impact Assessment
HIC	hydrogen-induced cracking
HIP	hot isostatic pressing
HIPO	high potential (incident) (I've also seen HiPo used, but HIPO seems to be preferred)
HIPPS	high-integrity pressure protection system (seems to be preferred, although high integrity pipeline protection system has also been used)
HIPS	high integrity protection system
HIST	host interoperability support test
HMA	half-strength mud acid
HMB	heat and material balance
HMI	human-machine interface
HMO	Health Maintenance Organization
HNBR	hydrogenated nitrile butadiene rubber
HOA	hand/off/auto (switch)
HOD	Head of Discipline
HoE	Head of Engineering
HOIS	Harwell offshore inspection (R&D) service
HOT	heavy oil tar
hp	horsepower

HP	Hewlett Packard Pressure Gauge
HP	high pressure
HP/HT	high pressure/high temperature
HP/LP	high pressure/low pressure
HPA	High Population Area
HPHT	high pressure, high temperature
HPJF	high-pressure jet flushing
HPRT	high-pressure recovery turbine
HPU	hydraulic power unit
HPV	hydrocarbon pore volume
HQ	Headquarters
hr	hour
HR	Human Resources
hr/d	hours per day
HRA	Health Risk Assessment
HRAS	Human Resources/Administrative Services
HRB	Rockwell hardness number, B scale, tested with a steel ball
HRC	Rockwell C Hardness
HRIS	Human Resources Information System
HRP	Human Resource Planning
HRR	Hazard and Risk Register
HRSG	Heat Recovery Steam Generator
HRVOC	highly reactive volatile organic compound
HS	identifier for a "high" frequency damper for secondary modes
HSB	hydrostatic bailer
HSC	hydrogen stress cracking
HSD	Hurl State Development
HSE	Health and Safety Executive (UK version of OSHA)
HSE	Health, Safety, and Environment)
HSE	health, safety, and environmental
HSE	high-speed Ethernet
HSEQ	Health, Safety, and Environmental Quality
HSET	Health, Safety, and Environment Team
HSM	horizontal support member
HSO_3	bisulfite ion
HSSE	health, safety, security, and the environment
HSSE&O	health, safety, security, environmental, and operational

HSSEE	Health, Safety, Security, Environment, and Engineering
HSST	hydraulic selective shifting tool
HT	high temperature
HTALHC	heavier than air light hydrocarbon
HTFS	Heat Transfer and Fluid Flow Service
HTML	hypertext markup language
HTP	hydrostatic test pressure
HTRI	Heat Transfer Research, Inc.
HUC	Hookup and Commissioning
HV	high voltage
HV	Vickers hardness
Hv_{10}	Vickers hardness measured with a 10 kgf indenter.
HVAC	heating, ventilating, and air conditioning
HVOF	high-velocity oxygen fuel
HVWF	high-velocity water flushing
HVY	heavy
HWO	hydraulic workover
HYCS	high yield carbon steel
HYD	hydraulic
Hz	hertz

I

i	ASME B31 Code stress intensification factor
I	hot service insulation
I&A	Integrity and Assurance
I&C	instrumentation and control
I&E	instrument and electrical
I&PS	Instrumentation and Protective Systems
I&T	Inspection and Test(ing)
I.D.	inside diameter
i.e.	id est (that is) always use with periods and comma, as in (i.e., xxx) (don't define)
I/O	input/output
I/P	current to pneumatic transducer
I/P	current to pressure converter
I2	negative sequence current
IA	inner annulus
IA	Inspection Authority
IA	Integrity Analyst

IACS	International Association of Certification Societies
IAEA	International Atomic Energy Agency
IAEI	International Association of Electrical Inspectors
IAM	Integrity Analyst Meeting
IAM	Integrity and Assurance Manager
IAP	Incident Action Plan
IAP	inner annulus pressure
IBC	intermediate bulk container
IBC	International Building Code
IBP	inflatable bridge plug
Ic	cold service
IC	Incident Commander
IC	initiating cause
IC	Inspection Coordinator
IC	Installation contractor
IC	internal concavity
ICBO	International Conference of Building Officials
ICC	International Code Council
ICDA	Internal Corrosion Direct Assessment
ICE	Instrument, Control, and Electrical
ICE	International Electrotechnical Commission
ICEA	Insulated Cable Engineers Association
IChemE	Institution of Chemical Engineers
ICL	initiating cause likelihood
ICM	inspection and corrosion management
ICM	inspection and corrosion monitoring
ICOR	Interprofessional Council on Registration
ICP	Incentive Compensation Plan
ICP	Incident Command Post
ICS	Incident Command System
ICS	Integrated Control System
ICSS	Integrated Control and Safety System
ID	identification
ID	induced draft
ID	inside diameter *(not internal diameter: and use I.D. for the acronym, not ID)*
IDAL	In-line Inspection Data Analysis Lead
IDC	initiating device circuit
IDLH	Immediately Dangerous to Life and Health

IEC	International Electrotechnical Commission (*note: watch for this being misdefined, such as International Electrochemical Commission*)
IEEE	Institute of Electrical and Electronics Engineers *(note: watch for this being misdefined as IEE, Institution of Electrical Engineers)*
IEL	intermediate event likelihood
IESNA	Illuminating Engineering Society of North America
IFA	Issued for Approval
IFB	insulating firebrick
IFB	Issued for Bid
IFC	International Fire Code
IFC	Issued for Construction (e.g., drawings)
IFD	Issued for Demolition
IFD	Issued for Design
IFGC	International Fuel Gas Code
IFP	Issued for Purchase
IFQ	Issued for Quote
IFR	Issued for Review
IFS	Integrated Field Scheduling
IGA	intergranular attack
IGE	Institution of Gas Engineers
IH	Industrial Hygienist
IIA	Independent Inspection Authority
IIE	Institute of Industrial Engineers
IIS	Internet Information Services
IIW	International Institute of Welding
IIWL	inter-island water line
IKB	interactive knowledge base
IL	integrity level
ILI	in-line inspection
IM	Integrity Management
IM/MAR	Integrity Management/Major Accident Risk
IMC	International Mechanical Code
IMF	Intermediate Manifold Facility
IMO	International Maritime Organization
IMP	Integrity Management Program *(also sometimes Integrity Management Plan)*
IMS	Incident Management System

IMT	Incident Management Team
IMU	Inertial Motion Unit
in.	inch *(spell out in text; use in. if needed in tables or figures only)*
in.wg.	inches of water gauge
in/ft	inch(es) per foot
in^2	square inch(es)
INC	increase
IND	Indicator
INS	Insulation Code
INS	Inertial Navigation System
IO	Information Officer
IOR	initial oil rate
IP	independent protection layer
IP	inflatable packer or intermediate pressure, *possibly also injection pump*
IP	ingress protection
IP	Inspection Planner
IP	Intermediate Pressure
IP	Internet protocol
IPA	initial participating area
IPC	International Plumbing Code
IPC	internal plastic coating
IPF	Instrumented Protective Function
IPL	independent protection layer
IPL	In-line Inspection Program Lead
IPLOCA	International Pipe Line and Offshore Contractors Association
IPS	inch(es) per second *(vibration measurement in velocity units)*
IPS	inspection performance suspect
IPS	Instrumented Protective System
IPSRS	Instrumented Protective System Requirements Specification
IPWHT	intermediate post-weld heat treatment *(also known as ISR Intermediate stress relief)*
IQ	inspection query
IQI	image quality indicator
IQM	Inspection and quality management

IQM	integrity and quality management
IR	Incident Report
IR	infrared
IR	insulation resistance
IR/UV	infrared/ultraviolet
IRA	Individual Retirement Account
IRC	Information Resource Center
IRIS	Internal Rotary Inspection System
IRN	Inspection Release Note
IRO	Incident Response Organization
IRP-1	Interdiscipline Review Process-1, 2 etc.
IRR	internal rate of return
IRS	Internal Revenue Service
IRT	Item Response Theory
IS	intrinsically safe
ISA	International Society of Automation *(formerly Instrumentation, Systems, and Automation Society; often misdefined as Instrumentation Society of America, Instrument, Systems, and Automation Society)*
ISASR	in support application supplied by applicant
ISD	inherently safer design
ISEA	International Safety Equipment Association
ISIP	initial shut-in pressure
ISO	Incentive Stock Option
ISO	International Organization for Standardization (NOT International Standards Organization)
ISO (drawings)	isometric
ISRS	integral stem, replaceable seats
ISRS	International Safety Rating System
ISSP	item-specific scoring plan
ISSSV	injection subsurface safety valve
IST	injection suction tank
IT&S	Information Technology and Services
ITE	Institute of Transportation Engineers
ITK	interoperability test kit
ITL	Inspection Team Lead
ITP	Inspection and Test Plan
ITS	Inspection Test Summary
ITT	Invitation to Tender

IU	internal undercut
IUD	instantaneous underbalance device
IVB	Independent Verification Body
IWE	International Welding Engineer
IWE	International Welding Technician
IWG	Initiative Work Group
IWL	Incomplete Work List
IWOCS	Intervention and Workover System
IWS	International Welding Specialist

J

J	joule
JB	junction box
JHA	Job Hazard Analysis
JIC	Joint Information Center
JIP	joint industry project
JIT	just-in-timeJMP Journey Management Plan
JOL	Jurisdiction On-Line (database)
JOP	Job Opportunity Program
JSA	Job Safety Analysis
JSA/JHA	Job Safety Analysis/Job Hazard Analysis
JSEA	Job Safety and Environmental Impact Analysis
JTTAS	Japanese Technology Transfer Association
JV	joint venture
JVA	Joint Venture Agreements

K

k	kilo
K	Kelvin (temperature scale)
k	thousand (kilo) k
kA	kilo-amperes
KB	Kelly Bushing
kbit/s	kilobits per second
KBS	knowledge-based systems
kcmil	1,000 circular mils
Kd	Derivative gain
Kdamper	the dynamic stiffness of an added damper
KEOR	Kellogg Enhanced Oil Recovery
keV	kiloelectron volt

kg	kilogram(s)
kg/cm^2	kilogram(s) per square centimeter
kg/hr	kilogram(s) per hour
kg/m^2	kilogram(s) per square meter
kg/m^3	kilogram(s) per cubic meter
kg/m-s^2	kilogram(s) per meter per square second
kg/s	kilogram(s) per second
kg/sec	kilogram(s) per second
kHz	kilohertz
Ki	integral gain
kJ	kilojoule
KJ	Knuckle Joint or Knuckle Jar
kJ/in	kilojoule per inch
kJ/mm	kilojoule per millimeter
km	kilometer
km/h	kilometers per hour
kN/m^2	kiloNewtons per square meter
KO	knockout
KOH	potassium hydroxide
Kp	proportional gain
kPa	kilopascal
kPag	kilopascals gauge
KPI	Key Performance Indicator
ksi	1,000 pounds per square inch (psi) (or kilopounds per square inch) *[some abbreviate definition to kips per square inch; we will use kilopounds per square inch)*
kV	kilovolt
kVA	kilovolt-ampere
kVAR.	kilovolt-amperes reactive
kW	kilowatt(s)
kW/m^2	kilowatt(s) per square meter
kWh	kilowatt-hour
L	
L	identifier for a "low" frequency damper for primary modes
L	liter
L/O	layout
L/R	launcher and receiver (pigging)

L/V	liquid/vapor ratio
L2RA	Level 2 Risk Assessment
LACT	lease automatic custody transfer
LAH	level alarm high
LAHH	level alarm high-high
LAN	Local Area Network
LAS	link active scheduler
lb	pound *(use in tables and figures only; spell out in text)*
lb/ft^2	pound per square foot
lb/ft^3	pound per cubic foot
lb/ft-s^2	pounds per foot per square second
lb/hr	pounds per hour
lbf	pound-force
lbf/in	pound-force per inch
lbf/in^2	pound-force per square inch
lb-ft	foot pound
lbs.	pounds
lbs/ft^3	pounds per cubic feet
LC	lethal concentration
LC	lethal concentration
LC	level controller
LC	locked closed
LCC	life-cycle costing
LCD	liquid crystal display
LCN	Local Control Network
LCS	local control station
LCU	lower cretaceous unconformity
LD	lay down
LD	lethal dose
LDAR	leak detection and repair
LDF	large-diameter flow line
LDF	lay down for night
LDR	land disposal restriction
LDS	leak detection system
LED	light-emitting diode
LEL	lower explosive limit
LER	Local Equipment Room
LFEC	low-frequency eddy current
LFIP	Long-term Frequent Inspection Program

LFL	lower flammability limit
LFWN	long forged-weld neck flange
LGL	Legal Officer
	low ground pressureLHV Lower Heating Value
LHV	luminite-hydrate-vermiculite
LIA	Lead Integrity Analyst
LIB	lead impression block
LIDAR	light detection and ranging
LIS	Land Information Systems
LM	link master
LME	liquid metal embrittlement
LNG	liquefied natural gas
LO	Liaison Officer
LO/LC	locked open/locked closed *(valves)*
LoC	Letter of conformity.
LOC	light oil column
LOMS	Local Operating Management System
LON	local operating network
LoP	Layer of Protection
LOPA	Layer of Protection Analysis
LOPC	loss of primary containment
LOSC	Local On-Scene Coordinator
LOSH	Limits of System Handover
LOT	leak-off test
LOTO	lockout/tagout
LP	linear program or programming
LP	low pressure
LPA	Lisburne Participating Area
LPC	Lisburne Production Center
LPE	liquid penetrant examination
LPG	liquefied petroleum gas
LPR	linear polarization resistance *(probe)*
LPS	low-pressure separation *(some companies use low-pressure system)*
LR	low rise
LR	long radius
LR	long range
LRB	low rise basement
LRGWUT	long-range guided wave ultrasonic testing or technology

LRP	long-range planning
LS	identifier for a "low" frequency damper for secondary modes
LS	Land Surveyor
LS	lump sum
LSC	Logistics Section Chief
LSI	Land Surveyor Intern
LSIT	Land-Surveyor-in-Training
LT	ladle treatment
LT	Leadership Team
LT	leak testing
LT	low temperature
LTA	lost time accident
LTC	low-temperature curing
LTD	long-term disability
LTI	lost time incident
LTRM	long term reservoir management
LTS	Ledcor Technical Services
LTS	low-temperature separation
LUB	lubricator
LUN	Livening up/Energization Notice
LV	low voltage
LVDT	linear variable differential transformers
LWD	logging while drilling
LY	low yield
LYCS	low-yield carbon steel

M

M or <u>M</u>	molar
M	identifier for a "medium" frequency damper for primary modes
m	meter
M	monthly
M	thousand
M&R	Maintenance and Reliability Team
mμ	millimicron
m/s	meter per second
m^2	square meter(s)
m^3	cubic meter

m^3/m^3	cubic meters per cubic meter
m^3/yr	cubic meters per year
MA	major accident
MA	Marine Authority
MA	matters arising
mA	milliamp
MA	Mud Acid
MAC	Main Automation Contractor
MAC	Management Advisory Committee
MACT	Maximum Achievable Control Technology
MAF	Main Area Facility
MAH	Major Accident Hazard
MAHA	Major Accident Hazard Analysis
MAOP	maximum allowable operating pressure
MAP	Materials Amendment Proposal
MAPD	Major Accident Prevention Document
MAPPS	Management Association for Private Photogrammetric Surveyors
MAR	Major Accident Risk
MARR	Major Accident Risk Review
MATP	maximum allowable transient pressure
MAWP	maximum allowable working pressure
MB	Main Building
MBA	Member Board Administrators
mbar	millibar
MBOS	model-based operational support
MBP	marked burst pressure
MBPC	model-based predictive control
MBPD	million barrels per day
mbpd	thousand barrels per day
MBR	monthly business report
MC	mechanical completion
MC	metal-clad
MC	metal-clad cable
MCA	Maritime and Coastguard Agency
MCB	miniature circuit breaker
MCC	Mobile Command Center or Motor Control Center or Main Construction Camp
MCCB	molded-case circuit breaker

MCM	multicell model
MCM	multichip module
MCS	Master Control Station
MD	measured depth
MDMT	minimum design metal temperature
MDOF	multidegree of freedom
MDPE	medium-density polyethylene
MDR	Material Degradation Report
MDT	minimum design temperature
MDT	Modular Dynamics Tester (logging tool provided by Schlumberger)
MEA	monoethanolamine
MEF	mitigated event frequency
MEG	monoethylene glycol
MEGGE	model evaluation guidelines for gas explosion
MEI	metal-enclosed interrupter (type of switchgear)
MEL	major equipment list
MEL	Master Equipment List
MEL	Mitigated Event Likelihood
meq	milliequivalent
MERT	Medical Emergency Response Team
MeV	million electron volts
MF	medium frequency
MFE	magnetic flux exclusion
MFL	magnetic flux leakage
MFP	manifold flowing pressure
MFS	module fabrication site
MFT	manifold flowing temperature
MFWF	midfield waterflood
mg	milligram
mg/kg	milligram per kilogram)
mg/L	milligram per liter
mgd	million gallons per day
MgO	magnesium oxide
MGS	major gas sales
MHz	megahertz
MI	MI Drilling Fluids Service Company
mi	mile (spell out instead)
MI	mineral insulated

MI	mineral wool insulated
MI	miscible injectant
MIA	Major Incident Announcement
MIC	microbiologically induced corrosion
MIC	microbiologically influenced corrosion
mil	milli-inch (use ml for milliliter, mil for milli-inch)
mils	milli-inches
MIMIR	Mechanical Integrity Management Information Repository
min.	minute (spell out in text; use abbreviation if needed in tables and figures only)
MIO	micaceous iron oxide
MIP	Maximum Incidental Pressure (same as MATP)
MIRL	medium intensity runway and taxiway lights
MIRU	move in rig up
MIS	Manufacturing Information System
MIV	Main Instrument Vendor
ML	silt *(USCS Group Symbol)*
ml	milliliter(s) (for liquid capacity; for gases, use cc)
ml/cm^2	milliliter(s) per square centimeter
MLLW	mean lower low water
MLW	mean low water
MM BTU/h	million British thermal units per hour
mm	millimeter(s)
MM	million
mm/y	millimeters per year
mm^2	square millimeters
MMCFD	million cubic feet per day
MMS	Maintenance Management System
MMS	Minerals Management Service
mmscfd	million standard cubic feet per day
Mn	manganese
Mn	generalized mass for mode number "n"
Mo	molybdenum
mo.	month
MOC	Main Operations Center
MODU	Mobile Offshore Drilling Unit
mol %	mole percent
mol wt	molecular weight

MOL	main oil line
MoM	Minutes of Meeting
MOP	maximum operating pressure
MOV	motor-operated valve
MP	Major Projects
mp	melting point
MPA	Major Project Authorization
MPa	megapascal(s)
MPC	Mobil Phillips Chevron
MPcp	Major Projects common process
MPFM	multiphase flow meter
mph	miles per hour
MPI	magnetic particle inspection
MPPL	Maintenance Pigging Program Lead
MPQT	Manufacturing Procedure Qualification Test
MPS	Manufacturing Procedure Specification
mps	meters per second
MPU	Milne Point Unit
mpy	mils per year
MR	material requisition
mR/hr	milliroentgen/hour
MRB	Manufacturing Record Book
MRD	Mutual Recognition Document
MRG	master reference ground
MS	Identifier for a "medium" frequency damper for secondary modes
ms	millisecond
mscfd	million standard cubic feet per day
mscfd	thousand standard cubic feet per day
MSDS	Material Safety Data Sheet
MSL	mean sea level *(5 feet MSL is above sea level; -5 feet MSL is below sea level)*
MSPS	Michigan Society of Professional Surveyors
MsS	magnetostrictive sensors
MSS	Manufacturers Standardization Society of the Valve and Fittings Industry
MST	Management Support Team
MSTR	master
MT	magnetic particle testing

MT	Mitigation Tracker
MTBF	mean time between failures
MTI	magnetic particle inspection
MTL	Maintenance Team Lead
MTQP	Manufacturing and Test Quality Plan
MTR	Material Test Report
MTR	motor
MTRT	manual tangential radiographic technique
MTTFS	mean time to fail spurious
MTTR	mean time to repair
MTW	machine-tool wire
MUT	manual ultrasonic testing
MV	medium voltage
MV	manipulated variable
MV	megavolt
mV	millivolts
MVA	megavolt ampere
MVC	multivariable control
MVPC	multivariable predictive control
MVPC/O	multivariable predictive control and optimization
MVR	manual voltage regulator
MW	megawatt
mW	milliwatt
MW	molecular weight
MWC	municipal waste combustor
MWD	measurements while drilling
MWO	Model Work Order
MWP	maximum working pressure

N

N or $\underline{N}$	normal (concentration)
N	nitrogen (use N_2?)
N	normal
N	number of stress reversals (cycles) to failure
N/A	not applicable
N/m^2	newton per square meter
N/mm^2	newton per square millimeter
N_2	nitrogen
NABIE	National Academy of Building Inspection Engineers

NAC	notification appliance circuit
NAC	naphthanic acid corrosion
NACE	NACE International *(formerly National Association of Corrosion Engineers International)*
NaCl	sodium chloride
NaClO$_2$	sodium hypochlorite
NAE	National Academy of Engineering
NAEC	naphthanic acid erosion corrosion
NAFE	National Academy of Forensic Engineers
NAFTA	North American Free Trade Agreement
NANA	Northwest Alaska Native Association
NaOH	sodium hydroxide
NAS	National Aerospace Standards
Nb	niobium
NB	nominal bore
NBIC	National Board Inspection Code
NBP	normal boiling point
NBR	acrylonitrile butadiene rubber
NCARB	National Council of Architectural Registration Boards
NCE	New Chemical Evaluation
NCEES	National Council of Examiners for Engineering and Surveying
NCIL	noncorrosion inspection location
NCN	Nonconformance Note
NCR	Nonconformance Report
NCS	No Credible Scenario
NCS	NANA Corporate Services
NCSEA	National Council of Structural Engineers Associations
NDC	NANA Development Corporation
NDE	nondestructive evaluation
NDE	nondestructive examination
NDT	nondestructive testing
NEC	National Electrical Code
NEEC	Nalco Exxon Energy Chemicals
NEMA	National Electrical Manufacturers Association
NESC	National Electrical Safety Code
NFPA	National Fire Protection Association
NGI	Natural Gas Injection (North Gas Injection pad)
NGL	natural gas liquid

NGO	nongovernmental organization
NH^3	ammonia
NI	National Instrument
Ni	nickel
NICE	National Institute of Ceramic Engineers
NICET	National Institute for Certification in Engineering Technologies
NIEE	National Institute for Engineering Ethics
NII	nonintrusive inspection
NIS	Not in Service
NLL	neutron lifetime log
NLRA	National Labor Relations Act
NLRB	National Labor Relations Board
Nm	nanometer
NM	Network Management
Nm^3	normal cubic meters
NMA	network management agent
NMgr	Network Manager
NMR	nuclear magnetic resonance
No.	number
NOC	Notice of Completion
NOP	next operational period
NOP	normal operating pressure
NOR	net oil rate
NORM	naturally occurring radioactive material
NORSOK	Norsk Offshore Sector Standard (Norwegian Technology Standards Institution)
NOx	nitrogen oxides
NP	New Projects Group
NPD	Norwegian Petroleum Directorate
NPDES	National Pollutant Discharge Elimination System
NPM	North Process Module
NPMS	National Pipeline Mapping System
NPREP	National Preparedness for Response Exercise Program
NPS	nominal pipe size
NPSH	net positive suction head
NPSHA	net positive suction head available
NPSHR	net positive suction head required
NPT	National Pipe Thread

NPV	net present value
NRC	NANA Regional Corporation (do not use; use NANA instead)
NRC	National Response Center
NRC	Nuclear Regulatory Commission
NRDA	Natural Resource Damage Assessment
NRTL	Nationally Recognized Testing Laboratory
NS	North Slope
NSAE	National Society of Architectural Engineers
NSB	North Slope Borough
NSCI	No Serious Consequence Identified
NS-CIC	North Slope Corrosion, Inspection, and Chemicals Team
NSCR	nonselective catalytic reduction
NSD	North Slope Directive
NSF	National Sanitation Foundation
NSOM	North Slope Operations Manager
NSPE	National Society of Professional Engineers
NSPS	National Society of Professional Surveyors
NSPS	New Source Performance Standard
NSRE	North Slope Reservoir Engineer
Nss	suction-specific speed
NSSRT	North Slope Spill Response Team
NST	Northstar
NSTC	North Slope Training Corporation
NSTDT	North Slope Training & Development Team
NSU	North Slope Unit
NT	new technology
NTIW	no tube in window
NUI	normally unmanned installation
NWFB	Northwest Fault Block
NWS	Northwest Schrader
NWT	nominal wall thickness

O

O&M	operations and maintenance (capitalize if a department or division; otherwise, lowercase)
O.D.	outside diameter
O/U	Owner/User
O_2	oxygen

OA	outer annulus
OAL	overall length
OAP	outer annulus pressure
°C	degrees Celsius
OC	On Scene Commander
OCR	original condensate reserve
OCS	Outer Continental Shelf (Offshore Regulations)
OCTG	Oil Country Tubular Goods (e.g., casing and tubing)
OCX	Operations Center expansion
ODBC	open database connectivity
ODE	opposite drive end
ODIE	Operations Document Information Exchange
ODPCP	Oil Discharge Prevention and Contingency Plan
OE	Optimization Engineer (could also be referred to as WOE or POE)
OEM	original equipment manufacturer
°F	degrees Fahrenheit
OFC	optical fiber conductive
OFCCP	Office of Federal Contract Compliance Programs
OFCD	optical fiber conductive for plenum or ducts
OFCG	optical fiber conductive general purpose
OFCR	optical fiber conductive for risers
OFF PAD	structures and equipment off-well-pad site
OFN	optical fiber nonconductive
OFND	optical fiber nonconductive for plenum or ducts
OFNG	optical fiber nonconductive general purpose
OFNR	optical fiber nonconductive for risers
OH	open hole
OI	On Injection (status)
OIAS	Operations Integrity Assurance System
OIES	Office of International Education Services (division of AACRAO)
OIM	Offshore Installation Manager
OIR	Offshore Incident Report
OISS	Operations Integrity Support Specialist
OJ	oil jars
OJT	on-the-job training
OL	online (status)
OL	organic silt, organic clay (USCS Group Symbol)

OLE	object linking and embedding
OMAR	Oil Movements Accounting and Reporting
OMER	Operations, Maintenance, and Emergency Response (manual)
OMS	Operating Management System
ON PAD	structures and equipment on-well-pad site
ONAF	Oil Natural Air Forced *(Note: electrical term; air conditioning)*
ONAN	Oil Natural Air Natural *(Note: electrical term; air conditioning)*
ONP	onshore pipeline
OOIP	original oil in place
OOS	out of service
OP	operating pressure
OP	output
OPA 90	Oil Pollution Act of 1990
OPA	Oil Pollution Act
OPA	Other Populated Area
OPB	occupied portable building
OPC DX	OPC for data exchange
OPC	offshore pipelines and causeways
OPCOLE	object linking and embedding for process control
OPC-UA	object linking and embedding (OLE) for process control – unified architecture
OPEX	operating expense or operational expenditure
OPGW	optical fiber ground wire
OPS	Office of Pipeline Safety
Ops	Operations
OQ	Operator Qualification (plan)
OREDA	Offshore REliability DAta *(note the odd use of caps is correct)*
ORP	oxidation reduction potential
ORT	operator response time
OS	Out of Service
OS	overshot
OS&D	Overage, Shortage, and Damage
OS&Y	outside stem and yoke (valve)
OSBL	outside battery limits
OSC	Operations Section Chief or Operations Subcommittee

OSD	operating shutdown
OSHA	Occupational Safety and Health Administration
OSM	Onshore Site Manager
OSM	Office of Surface Mining
OSP	Outside Plant
OSRO	Oil Spill Removal Organization
OT	overtime
OTDP	Operations Training Development Program
OTDT	Operations Training Development Team
OTI	Offshore Technology Information
OTL	oil transit line
OTL	Operations Team Leader
OTS	operator training simulator
OU	Owner/User
OVP	Operations Value Process
OWC	oil water contact
oz	ounce (spell out in text)
oz/ft^2	ounces per square foot
oz/ft^3	ounces per cubic foot

P

P	pressure
P	personnel protection
P	pipe internal pressure
P	proportional
P&I	piping and instrument
P&ID	piping and instrumentation diagram; NOTE: Can also be process and instrumentation diagram
p.	page
P.E.	Professional Engineer
p.m.	post meridian (afternoon)
P.O.	Purchase Order
P.O.D.	probability of detection
P/N	part number
P/S	publisher/subscriber
P/S	weekly report of Staff Production/Safety Engineer
PA	Performance Appraisal
PA	Phased Array
PA	power amplifier

PA	Public Address (system)
PAC	Physical Acoustics Corporation
PACR	predicted average cracking ratio
PAFA	Process Area Fire Alarm
PAH	pressure alarm high
PAI	Phillips Alaska, Inc.
PAIT	Pipeline Assessment and Intervention Team
PAKS	Professional Activities and Knowledge Study
PAL	pressure alarm low
PAL	Production/Artificial Lift
PAPI	precision approach path indicator
PAR	preassembled pipe racks
PARLOC	pipeline and riser loss of containment database
PAS	pressurized air shock
PAS	process automation system
PAU	preassembled units
PAW	plasma arc welding
Pb	lead
PB	pump bailer
PBE	plain both ends
PBFM	Prudhoe Bay Field Manager
PBLC	Prudhoe Bay Location Code
PBOC	Prudhoe Bay Operations Center
PBR	polished bore receptacle
PBRE	Prudhoe Bay Reservoir Engineer
PBU	Prudhoe Bay Unit or pressure buildup
Pburst	Predicted Burst Pressure
PC	personal computer or pressure controller or Production Coordinator
PCB	polychlorinated biphenyl
PCC	process computer control or Production Control Center or planning, commercial, and control
PCDP	Public Consultation and Disclosure Plan
PCDS	process control digital security
PCE	Project Control Engineer
pcf or lb/ft³	pounds per cubic foot
PCHE	printed circuit heat exchanger
PCI	Precast/Prestressed Concrete Institute
PCM	parameter crack measurement

P_{CM}	cracking parameter (Ito-Bessyo formula)
PCM	Project Change Management
PCM	power control module
PCN	Personnel Certification in Nondestructive Testing
PCN	Process Change Notice
PCN	process control network
PCP	pipeline competent person
Pcp	Projects Common Process (R&M)
PCR	Problem-Cause-Remedy
PCR	process change request
PCS	process control strategy
PCS	process control system
PCT	production combination tool
PCTF	Production Capacity Task Force
PCV	pressure control valve
PD	pressure drop
PD	proportional derivative
PDAM	Pipeline Defect Assessment Manual
PDF	Portable Document Format
PDG	Personal Development Guide
PDMS	Plant Design Management System (software package)
PDP	Personal Development Plan
PDS	Pipeline Data Sheet
PDS	Power Distribution System
PE	Petroleum Engineer
PE	plain end
PE	polyethylene
PE	Principles and Practice of Engineering exam
PE	Production Engineer
PE.	Project Engineer
PEC	pulsed eddy current
PECS	packaged equipment control system
PED	Pressure Equipment Directive
PEEK	polyetheretherketone
PEP	Project Execution Plan
PERC	powered emergency release coupling
percent	% (*in tables, spell out in text*)
PES	programmable electronic system
PES	Production Engineering Supervisor

PES	programmable electronic system
PET	Process Evaluation Team
PEX	cross-linked polyethylene
PFD	probability of failure on demand
PFD	process flow diagram
PFHE	plate-fin heat exchanger
PFO	pressure falloff
PFP	passive fire protection
pg	design ground snow load in psf (lbs per square feet)
P-GMAW	pulsed gas metal arc welding
PH	precipitation hardened
PHA	Process Hazard Analysis
PHA/PSA	Process Hazard Assessment/Process Safety Assessment
PHAST	Process Hazard Analysis software tool
PHMSA	Pipeline and Hazardous Materials Safety Administration
PHSER	Project Health, Safety, and Environmental Review
PHSSER	Project Health, Safety, Security, and Environmental Review
PI	pressure indicator
PI	Productivity Index
PI	proportional integral or process information
PIC	person in charge
PIC	pressure indicating controller
PID	proportional-integral-derivative (controller)
PIMS	Pipeline Integrity Management System
PIN	process information network
PIP	Performance Incentive Plan
PIP	Process Industry Practices (USA)
PITS	Pump in Temperature Survey
PKR	packer
pl	picoliter
PL	punchlist
PL	pipeline
PL	Project Leader
PL	protection layer
PLC	programmable logic controller
PLE	plain large end
PLE/TSE	plain large end/threaded small end
PLEM	pipeline end manifolds

PLET	pipeline end termination
PLL	potential loss of life
PLS	Professional Land Surveyor
PM	partner meeting (as in joint venture partners) .
PM	Performance Management
PM	Photomultiplier Tube
PM	Planned Maintenance
PM	Portfolio Manager
PM	Preventive Maintenance (cap if part of official program as in Preventive Maintenance Program procedures) - also note, preventive, not preventative
PM	Production Manager
PM	progress meeting
PM	Project Manager
PM10	particulate matter 10 micrometers or less in diameter
PM2.5	particulate matter 2.5 micrometers or less in diameter project management contractor
PMF	Production Maintenance Facilities
PMG	permanent magnetic generator
PMI	positive materials identification
PMI	Project Management Institute
PMP	Piping Modification Process *(note: not Plan or Package)*
PMR	Planned Maintenance Routine (a job plan)
PMR	process modification request
PMT	Project Management Team
PNL	pulsed neutron log
PNO	Profibus International
PO	processed oil
PO	Purchase Order (should not be PO but P.O. instead)
POB	Personnel on Board
POC	price of conformance
POD	probability of detection
PODS	Pipeline Open Data Standard
POE	plain one end
POE	probability of exceedance
POE	Production Optimization Engineer
POFR	plenum optical fiber raceway
POH	pull out of hole
POHC	principal organic hazard constituent

POI	probability of identification
POLC	Participating Organizations Liaison Council
POM	public opinion message
PONC	price of nonconformance
POP	Put On Production
POQR	Purchase Order Quality Requirements
PORV	pilot-operated relief valve
POS	probability of sizing
POW	Prudhoe Operations Warehouse
pp	pages
PP	Professional Policy (from the NCEES Manual of Policy and Position Statements)
PP	pulling prong
PPA	Pressure Point Analysis
ppb	parts per billion
ppbv	parts per billion by volume
PPD	pore pressure detection
PPE	personal protective equipment
PPFG	pore pressure fracture gradient
PPG	pounds per gallon
ppm	parts per million
PPM	Production/Inspection Meeting
ppmv	parts per million by volume
PPO	Preferred Provider Organization
PPP	pore pressure prediction
pPQR	preliminary Procedure Qualification Record
PPR	post-project review
ppt	parts per thousand
PQR	Procedure Qualification Record
PRBS	pseudo random binary sequence
PRCI	Pipeline Research Council International
PREN	pitting resistance equivalent
PRESS	pressure
PREw	pitting resistance equivalent number
PRF	produced oil fluid
PRIDE	Process Reporting Information and Data Entry
PRO	Pig Run Operation
PROC	procedure
PROJ	project

PROP	Pig Run Operation Plan
PRS	pressure reduction station
PRV	pressure relief valve
PS	Position Statement (from the NCEES Manual of Policy and Position Statements)
PS	process safety
PS	pump station
PS/IM	process safety/integrity management
PSA	Process Safety Assessment
PSA	production sharing agreement
PSA/PHA	Process Safety Assessment/Process Hazard Analysis
Psafe	safe operating pressure
PSC	Planning Section Chief
PSC	Planning Subcommittee
PSCM	procurement and supply chain management
PSD	process shutdown
PSE	plain small end
PSE	pressure safety element (i.e., ruptured disk)
PSE	Process Safety Engineer
psf or lb/ft^2	pounds per square foot
PSH	pressure switch high
psi	pounds per square inch
PSI	process safety information
psia	pounds per square inch absolute
psig	pounds per square inch gauge
PSL	pressure switch low
PSL	product specification level
PSM	Process Safety Management (sometimes defined as Project Safety Management, but *should* be Process)
PSME	process safety minimum expectation
PSR	Project Status Report
PSR	Project Safety Review
PSS	process safety system
PSSR	Prestart-up Safety Review
PST	primary separation tank
PSV	platform supply vessel
PSV	pressure safety valve
PT	liquid or dye-penetrant testing
Pt	peat (USCS Group Symbol)

pt	pint
PT	platinum
PT	power transformer
PT	pressure test
PT	pressure transducer
PT	pressure transmitter
pt/mmscfd	pint per million standard cubic feet per day
PTA	purified terephthalic acid
PTC	positive temperature coefficient
PTFE	polytetrafluoroethylene (Teflon®)
PTO	Permit to Operate
PTS	pressure temperature survey
pts/ft^2	(drip) points per square foot
pts/m^2	(drip) points per square meter
PTW	Permit to Work
PU	Performance Unit
PUL	Performance Unit Leader
PV	pressure control valve
PV	process measurement (e.g., temperature, pressure, etc.)
PV	process variable
PVC	polyvinyl chloride
PVD	pipeline vibration damper
PVDF	polyvinylidene difluoride
PVR	pressure vacuum relief
PVT	pressure, volume, and temperature (fluid properties)
PW	produced water
PWC	preferential weld corrosion
PWD	produced water drum
PWH	produced water handling
PWHT	post-weld heat treatment
PWHTmax	longest time for which the vessel may be heat treated
PWHTmin	shortest time for which the vessel may be heat treated to meet code requirements
PWI	produced water injection
PWR	project work release
PWT	production water treatment
PWX	produced water expansion
PWZ	peripheral wedge zone

Q

Q	quarter
Q&A	question and answer
Q&T	quenched and tempered (supply condition for some line pipe)
QA	quality assurance
QA/QC	quality assurance/quality control
QAP	Quality Assurance Plan
QAR	Quality Assurance Representative
QC	quality control
QCP	Quality Control Plan
QFR	Quarterly Financial Review
QL	quality level
QM	quality management
QMS	Quality Management System
QP	quadratic programming
QP	Quality Plan (some companies use this for quality program)
QPR	Quarterly Performance Review
QR	Quality Rating
QRA	Quantified Risk Assessment
QRA	quantified risk assessment
QRA	quantitative risk analysis
QRA	Quantitative Risk Assessment (some companies use it for Quantitative Risk Analysis)
QSV	Quality Surveillance Verification
qt	quart

R

R&D	research and development
R&M	refining and marketing
R&M Pcp	Refining and Marketing Segment Projects common process
R&M	reliability and maintainability
Ra	roughness average
RACI	responsible/accountable/consulted/informed
RAD	Reliability Assurance Document
RAM	random access memory
RAM	Reliability, Availability, and Maintainability (analysis)
RAP	Retirement Accumulation Plan

RAPID	Relative Assessment of Piping Integrity Data
RAS	requirement at site (procurement on site)
RAT	Remote Access Technology
RAZ	Restricted Access Zone
RAZOR	Reservoir Analysis Zone One Romeo
RB	resource block
RBA	risk-based assessment
R_{bend}	Radius of uninsulated pipe overbend corresponding to screening level bending strain: $R_{bend} = (D/2)/\varepsilon_s$
RBI	risk-based inspection
RC	recessed face
RCAC	Regional Citizens Advisory Council
RCF	refractory ceramic fiber
RCFA	Root Cause Failure Analysis
RCI	Reservoir Characterization Instrument (logging tool, provided by Baker Atlas)
RCP	resistor controlled cathodic protection
RCP	resin-coated proppant
RCRA	Resource Conservation and Recovery Act
RD	rig down
RDC	Remote Data Collector
RDFN	rig down for night
RDMO	rig down moved off
RDT	Reservoir Description Tool (logging tool provided by Halliburton)
Re	Reynolds number
RE	rotating equipment
RED	restriction enhancement drill (underreamer)
REI	Rotating Equipment Initiative
RE-IFC	Reissued for Construction
REIL	runway end identifier light
REQ	Requisition
RES SURV	reservoir surveillance
REV	Revision
RF	radio frequency
RF	raised face
RF	risk factor
RFI	radio frequency interference
RFI	Ready for Inspection

RFI	Request for Information
RFP	Request for Proposal
RFQ	Request for Quote
RFSF	raised face smooth finish
RFT	repeat formation tester
RGE	rich gas equivalents
RGS	rigid steel conduit
RH	relative humidity
RHA	Rivers and Harbors Act
RHO	radiant heat output
RHU	residue hydrotreater unit
RI H	running in hole
RIF	reduction in force
RIH	run in hole
RIK	replacement in kind
R_{ins}	Insulated radius corresponding to R_{bend}: $R_{ins} = R_{bend} + D/2 + t_{ins}$
RJ	USE RTJ INSTEAD: ring joint, a.k.a. ring-type joint (RTJ)
RKB	Reference Kelly Bushing
RLA	Remnant Life Assessment
RLE	Run Length Encoded Bitmap
RLG	Resource and Logistic Group
RM&D	remote monitoring and diagnostics
RMP	Risk Management Plan
RMP	Risk Management Program
RMS	root mean square
RO	restriction orifice
RO	repair order
ROC	rapid opening closure
ROE	radius of exposure
ROFR	riser optical fiber raceway
ROI	return on investment
ROM Cost	relative order of magnitude cost
ROM	read only memory
ROM	rough order of magnitude (+/- 50%)
ROT	remotely operated tool
ROV	remotely operated vehicle
ROV	rollover valve

ROW	right-of-way
RP	Recommended Practice
RP	Reliability Plan
RPD	Register of Protective Devices
RPM	remote performance management
rpm	revolutions per minute
RPRG	Reservoir Performance Review Group
RPT	rapid phase transition
RR	Risk Rank
RRB	Records Retention Board
RRF	risk reduction factor
RSG	Reservoir Study Group
RSPL	Recommended Spare Part List
RSRD	Register of Safety-related Devices
RSTRENG	remaining strength of corroded pipe
RSV	Reservoir Surveillance Group
RT	radiographic testing
RT	round trip
RTAP	real-time architecture project
RTD	resistance temperature detector/device
RTJ	ring-type joint
RTNS	returns
RTR	real-time radiography
RTRP	reinforced thermosetting resin piping
RTRT	real-time radiographic testing
RTU	remote terminal unit
RTU	remote transmission unit
RTV	rubber-tired vehicle
RU	rig up
RV	relief valve
RVI	remote visual inspection
RWO	rig workover

S

s	nominal stress range
s	seconds
S	Strouhal number
S.E.	Structural Engineer
S1	mapped earthquake spectral response acceleration for a

	1-second period as determined in the IBC 2006, Section 1613.5.1 and ASCE 7-05, Section 11.4.1, expressed as a percent of gravity (%g)
SAE	Society of Automotive Engineers
SAM	Staging Area Manager
SAM	subsea accumulator module
SAME	Society of American Military Engineers
SAP	segmentation application point
SAP	service access point
SAP	service advertising protocol
SAP	survivable adaptive planning
SAR	Stock Appreciation Rights Standard Air Ratio
SARA	Superfund Amendments and Reauthorization Act
SAT	safety analysis tables
SAT	Site Acceptance Test(ing)
SAW	submerged arc welded/welding
SB	small-bore iping
SB	screwed bonnet
SBHT	static bottom hole temperature
SBP	specified burst pressure
SBR	state board representative
SBU	Strategic Business Unit
SBV	subsurface barrier valve
SC	source control
SC	storage containers
SC	safety critical
SCADA	Supervisory Control and Data Acquisition
SCBA	self-contained breathing apparatus
SCC	secondary combustion chamber
SCC	stress corrosion cracking
SCDM	safety critical design measure
SCE	safety critical equipment (equipment, not environment)
SCEWO	safety critical equipment work order
scf	standard cubic foot/feet
scf/stb	standard cubic foot per stock tank barrel
scfh	standard cubic feet per hour
scfm	standard cubic feet per minute
SCH	schedule
SCIS	subsea chemical injection system

SCM	subsea control module
SCMMB	subsea control module mounting base
SCP	sustained casing pressure
SCR	selective catalytic reduction
SCR	steel catenary riser
SCRD	screwed
SCS	subsea control system
SCSSV	surface controlled subsurface safety valve
SCT	safety-critical task
SCWI	Senior Certified Welding Inspector
SD	shutdown
SD	standard deviation
SDA	spray dryer absorber
SDE	Spatial Database Engine
SDI	Steel Door Institute
SDOF	single degree of freedom
SDPU	subsea data processing unit
SDR	Supplier Deviation Request
SDRL	Suppliers Document Requirements Listing
SDS	system design specification
SDU	subsea distribution unit
SDV	shutdown valve
SE	screwed end
SE	Specifying Engineer
SE	standard error of the mean
SEAOC	Structural Engineers Association of California
sec or s	second (spell out in text)
SEM	scanning electron microscopy
SEM	subsea electronics module
SENB	single edge notched bend
SEO	shift exchange off
SER	sequence of events recorder
SERVS	Ship Escort/Response Vessel System
SESD	selective emergency shutdown
SEW	shift exchange work(ed)
SFF	safe failure fraction
SFPE	Society of Fire Protection Engineers
SG	specific gravity
SH	system handover

SI	International System of Units/System International d'Unites
SI	Shut-In (status)
Si	silicon
SI	Surveyor Intern
SIBHP	shut-in bottom-hole pressure
SIC	Standard Industrial Classification
SIE	Senior Inspection Engineer
SIF	safety-instrumented function
SIL	Safety Integrity Level
SIMMS	single inline memory modules
SIMOPS	simultaneous operations – drilling and construction or operations and construction
SIMS	Structural Integrity Management System
SINTAP	Structural Integrity Assessment Procedure
SIP	Seawater Injection Plant
SIRP	Safe Isolation and Reinstatement Practice
SIS	Safety Instrumented System
SISO	single-input, single-output
SIT	Surveyor-in-Training
SIT	Systems Integration Test
SITHP	shut-in tubing head pressure
SITP	shut-in tubing pressure or shut-in wellhead pressure
SIWHP	shut-in wellhead pressure or shut-in tubing pressure
SLB	strength-level blast
SLC	signaling line circuit
SLD	single-line drawing
SLE	strength-level event
SLI	safe load indicator
SLOD	significant likelihood of death
SLOFEC	saturated low frequency eddy current
SLOT	significant level of toxicity
SLOT	specified level of toxicity
SLRP	strategic long-range planning
SLS	Shared Learning System
SM	silty sand (USCS Group Symbol)
SM	system management
SMA	secondary muster area
SMA	Segment Marine Authority

SMACNA	Sheet Metal and Air Conditioning Contractors' National Association
SMAW	shielded metal arc welding
SMC	Strategic Management of Change
SME	Society for Mining, Metallurgy, and Exploration, Inc.
SME	Society of Manufacturing Engineers
SME	Subject Matter Expert
SMLS	seamless (as in seamless pipe)
SMOG	standardized measure of oil and gas
SMS	Sort Message Service
SMS	Safety Management System
SMUT	Shale Mapping Unit Task Force
SMYS	specified minimum yield stress – *the minimum stress specified at which the pipe material will plastically yield (If the writer means maximum instead, use MAOP*
SNAME	Society of Naval Architects and Marine Engineers
SNSP	Self Nomination Separation Program
SO	Safety Officer (IMT)
SO	shear out sub
SO	slip-on flange
SO_2	sulfur dioxide
SO_3	sulfur trioxide
SOC	Safety Observation and Conversation
SOE	sequence of events
SOHIC	stress-orientated hydrogen-induced cracking
SOL	safe operating limit
SOL	sockolet
SOP	Site Operating Procedure
SOP	Standard Operating Procedure
SOR	Serious Occurrence Report
SOR	Statement of Requirements
SORA	Safety Override Risk Assessment
SOSC	State On-Scene Coordinator
SOSS	standard oil surface simulator
SOV or SO	screened orifice valve (gas lift)
SOV	solenoid-operated valve
SOW	Scope of Work
SO_X	sulfur oxides
sp gr	specific gravity

SP	set point
SP/SE	Staff Production/Safety Engineer
SPA	Single Point of Accountability
SPA-CM	Single Point of Accountability for Corrosion Management
SPA-IM	Single Point Accountable for Integrity Management
SPC	statistical process control
SPC	Specification
SPCCP	Spill Prevention, Control, and Countermeasure Plan
SPCU	Subsea Power and Communications Unit
SPD	surge protection device
SPE	Society of Petroleum Engineers
SPE	Senior Petroleum Engineer
SPFU	smart pig follow-up
SPIG	smart pig
SPIKEYS	device worn on shoes to avoid slipping on ice
SPL	sound pressure level
SPL	Special Projects Lead
SPM	South Process Module
SPM	Strategy and Planning Manager
SPM	Supplier Performance Management
SPO/SPOC	single point of contact
SPPS	sand production pipe saver
SPR	Semiannual Performance Review
SPS	Subsea Production System
SQL	standard query language
SQP	sequential quadratic programming
SQP	System Quality Plan
SR	safe refuge
SR	short radius
SRA	safety-related alarm
SRA	Structural Reliability Analysis
SRAP	Supplemental Retirement Accumulation Plan
SRB	sulfate-reducing bacteria
SRK	Soave-Redlich-Kwong
SRS	Safety Requirement Specification
SRT	Spill Response Team
SRTF	Spill Reduction Task Force
SS TRIM	stainless steel trim

SS	mapped earthquake spectral response acceleration for short periods as determined in the IBC 2006, Section 1613.5.1 and ASCE 7-05, Section 11.4.1, expressed as a percent of gravity (%g)
SS	Sliding Sleeve
SS	stainless steel
SS	subsea
SSA	Shared Service Aviation
SSB	scope, schedule, and budget
SSC	sulfide stress cracking
SSCC	sulfide stress corrosion cracking
SS-FCAW	self-shielded flux-cored arc welding
SSIV	subsea isolation valve
SSM	subsurface maintenance
SSN	Social Security number
SSO	Site Safety Officer (TRT)
SSPC	Steel Structures Painting Council
SSPC	Society for Protective Coatings
SSSV	subsurface safety valve
SSTT	subsea test tree
SSV	surface safety valve
ST	steam heat-traced insulation service
ST	Strike Team
STB	stock tank barrel
STC	sound transmission class
STD	short-term disability
STEL	short-term exposure limit
STI	selectable timed interrupt
STI	Steel Tank Institute
STM1	synchronous transmission mode with bandwidth capacity up to 155 Mbps
STOBD	stock tank oil barrels per day
STP	Site Technical Practice
STP	spin/temp/pressure survey
SWTP	Seawater Treatment Plant
STV	standard treatment valve
STV	stock tank vapor
STX	steam exchanger
SU&C	Start-up and Commissioning for Operations

SUS	Saybolt Universal Seconds
SUT	Single Unit Testing
SUTA	Subsea Umbilical Termination Assembly
SVA	security vulnerability assessment.
SVI	single valve isolation
SW	seawater
SW	socket weld
SW	spiral-wound (gasket)
SW	stud welding
SW/SCR	socket weld / screwed
SW/SV	single-wall/single-image technique
SW/THRD	socket weld/threaded
SWB	seal-welded bonnet
SWC	sidewall core
SWC	stepwise cracking
SWE	single-wall examination
SWG	Standard Wire Gauge
SWG	swage
SWI	seawater injection
SWL	safe working load
SWMU	Solid Waste Management Unit
SWO	Standing Work Order
SWP	seawater plant, but use SWTP instead.
SWPPP	Stormwater Pollution Prevention Plan
SWS	Schlumberger Wellsite Services
SWSI	single wall single image
SWTP	Seawater Treatment Plant
SWV	single-wall viewing
SYS	System
SZC	soft zone cracking

T

T	ambient air temperature
t	pipe wall thickness
t	(tube wall) thickness
t	wall thickness
T&C	threaded and coupled
T&G	tongue and groove
T90	time to reach 90% of scale

TA	Technical Authority
TA	Travel Authorization or Technical Assistant
TAC	Technology Accreditation Commission
TAN	Total Acid Number
TAPS	Trans-Alaska Pipeline System
TAR	turnaround
TAs	Technical Authorities
Tau	Process time constant
TB	transducer block
TBD	To Be Determined
TBE	threaded both ends
TCCC	transfer of care, custody, and control
TCLP	Toxic Characteristic Leachate Procedures
TCO	total cost of ownership
TCP	transmission control protocol
TCP/IP	transmission control protocol/Internet protocol
TCV	toxicity characteristic
Td	derivative time
TD	design temperature
td	process dead time
TD	total depth
TD	tubing displacement
TDS	total dissolved solids
TDT	thermal decay tool
TDW	T.D. Williamson
te	metric ton (tonne)
TE	threaded end
TEACC	turbine-engine analysis compressor code
TeD	Technical Directorate
TEF	target event frequency
TEFC	totally enclosed, fan-cooled
TEG	triethylene glycol
TEL	tubing end locator
TEMA	Tubular Exchanger Manufacturers Association, Inc.
temp	temperature (tables only)
TEMPSC	totally enclosed motor-propelled survival craft
TEWAC	totally enclosed water-to-air-cooled
TF	Task Force
TF	Teflon® *[Use PTFE instead, or Teflon®]*

TFEP	tetrafluoroethylene polymer
THA	Task Hazard Assessment
THD	threaded
THHN	thermoplastic high heat-resistant nylon-coated
THK	thick
THRO	through
Ti	Integral time
TI	technical integrity
TI	temperature indicator
Ti	titanium
TI	turbulence intensity equal to the ratio of the RMS wind speed to the mean wind speed
TIA	Telecommunications Industry Association
TIC	total installed cost (+/-20 − +25%)
TIF	Tagged Image File
TIH	trip in hole
t_{ins}	insulation thickness
TL	Team Lead
TLC	top of line corrosion
TLE	thread large end
TLP	tension leg platform
TLV	threshold limit value
TMCP	thermomechanical controlled processing
TMEL	target mitigated event likelihood
TMS	Minerals, Metals, and Materials Society
TMTD	true mean temperature difference
TNO	The Netherlands Organization for Applied Scientific Research
TOC	table of contents
TOC	top of cement
TOE	threaded one end
TOFD	time-of-flight diffraction
TOL	takeoff/landing
TOL	threadolet
tonne	metric ton or tonne
TOR	Terms of Reference
TOS	top of Sadlerochit
TOS	Top of Steel
TP	tubing pressure or wellhead pressure

tpd	tons per day
TPE	thermoplastic elastomer
TPI	third-party inspector
TPI	third-party inspection/inspector
TPO	Treatment Plant Operator
TPY	tons per year
TQ	Technical Query
TQM	Total Quality Management
TR	Technical Reviewer
TR	temporary refuge
TRAP	Technical Risk Assurance Process
TRT	Tactical Response Team
TRT	tangential radiographic testing (*Note: sometimes technique is used instead of testing, but testing is preferred*)
TS	tapered swage
TS	tensile strength
TS	Tool Services
TSA	thermal spray aluminium
TSE	threaded small end
TSL	total sales liquids
TSS	total suspended solids
TT	tubing tail
TTE	time to event
TTLA	tank truck loading area
TUTA	Topside Umbilical Termination Assembly
TÜV	Technischer Überwachungsverein (Technical Inspection Organizations)
TVA	tuned vibration absorber
TVD	true vertical depth
TVP	Technology Vice President
TWA	time-weighted average
TWC	two-way check
TWI	The Welding Institute (UK)

U	
U	wind speed
U.S.	United States
U.S.C.	United States Code

UAA	University of Alaska Anchorage
UAF	University of Alaska Fairbanks
UBC	Uniform Building Code
UC	unified command
UCR	usual, customary, reasonable charge (medical charge)
UDC	underdeposit corrosion
UEL	upper explosive limit
UFC	Uniform Fire Code
UFL	upper flammability limit
UHF	ultra-high frequency
UIC	underground injection control
UK	United Kingdom
UKCS	United Kingdom Continental Shelf
UKOOA	United Kingdom Offshore Operators Association
UL	Underwriters Laboratories, Inc.
UL	Unit Leader
ULSD	ultra-low sulfur diesel
UNC	Unified National Course
UNF	Unified National Fine
UNS	Unified Numbering System
UOC	Unit Operators cost
UPC	Uniform Plumbing Code
UPDT	update
UPLG	Uniform Procedures and Legislative Guidelines (standing committee)
UPS	uninterruptible power supply *(note: often misdefined as uninterruptible power source, uninterruptible power system)* or United Parcel Service
UR	underreamer
UR	Utilization Review
URF	umbilicals, risers, and flow lines
US	upstream
US	Utilities Supervisor
USA	Unusually Sensitive Area
USACE	U.S. Army Corps of Engineers
USC	United States Code
USCG	United States Coast Guard
USCIEP	United States Council for International Engineering Practice

USCS	United Soil Classification System
USCS	United States Customary System
USNRC	United States Nuclear Regulatory Commission
USPLS	U.S. Public Lands Survey
UST	underground storage tank
USTS	U.S. Travel Service
UT	ultrasonic testing (not tested or technique)
UT	uniaxial tension
UTA	Umbilical Termination Assembly
UTM	Universal Transverse Mercator
UTS	ultimate tensile strength
UT-S	UT surface wave
UT-SW	UT shear wave
UT-TM	UT thickness measurement
UV	ultraviolet
UVCE	unconfined vapor cloud explosion
UXO	unexploded ordnance
V	
v	actual velocity
V	actual velocity
V	fluid velocity
V	vanadium
V	volt(s)
V/Hz	volts per hertz
V/L	vapor/liquid ratio
v/v	volume per volume
VA	volt-ampere
VAC	volts alternating current *(sometimes V.a.c. is used; use VAC instead)*
VAR	voltage adjustment rheostat
VCE	vapor cloud explosion
VCR	videocassette recorder
VCR	virtual communication relationship
VDC	Vendor Document Control
VDC	volts direct current (Not Vdc., but the latter is used sometimes. CHANGE IT TO VDC)
VDDR	Vendor Drawing and Data Requirements (not: Vendor Data and Documentation Requirement?)
VDU	vacuum distillation unit

VDU	visual (or video) display unit (i.e., computer monitor)
V_e	erosional velocity
ve	erosional velocity
VESDA	very early smoke detection apparatus
VEVRAA	Vietnam Era Veteran's Rehabilitation Assistance Act (of 1974)
VFD	virtual field device
VHF	very high frequency
VIP	Value Improving Practices
VMS	Vehicle Maintenance Shop
VND	vendor
VOC	volatile organic compound
VOD	vacuum oxygen decarbonization
VOL	volatile organic liquid
vol%	volume percent
VP	Verification Plan
VP	Vice President
VPC	volts per cell
VPI	vacuum pressure impregnation
VPI	vapor phase inhibitor
VPN	virtual private network
VROM	very rough order of magnitude
vs.	versus (tables only; spell out otherwise)
VSD	variable speed drive
VSM	vertical support member
VT	video teleconferencing
VT	visual testing
VT	voltage transformer
VTA	vacation travel allowance
VTA	vendor to advise

W

W	watt(s)
W	weekly
w.t.	wall thickness
W/ft	watts per foot
W/in^2	watts per inches squared
w/v	weight per volume
WA	Witness Authority

WAG	water alternating gas
WB	welded bonnet
WBS	work breakdown structure
WC	water cut
WCLIB	West Coast Lumber Inspection Bureau
WCRP	Well Control Response Plan
Wdamper	the weight of an added damper
WDSG	Well Damage Study Group
WE	weld end
WETS	Wellwork Economic Tracking System
WEV	weighted expectation value
WF	waterflood
WFMT	wet fluorescent magnetic particle testing
WG	wire grab
WGI	west gas injection
WGM	Works General Manager
WHP	wellhead pressure or tubing pressure
WHPU	Workover Hydraulic Power Unit
W-hr	watt-hour
WHRU	Waste Heat Recovery Unit
WIMS	Well Integrity Management System
WIN	Weld Identification Number
WIO	Working Interest Owners
WIP	Work in Progress
WIV	wind-induced vibration
WK2	rotational inertia
WL	well line
WLC	weight loss coupon
WLM	wireline measurement
WMF	Waste Management Facility
WN	weld neck
wo	distributed weight per unit length of pipe (includes pipe, contents, insulation and jacket)
WO	work order
WO	workover
WO	wrench operated
WOA	Western Operating Area
WOAD	Worldwide Offshore Accident Databank
WOE	Wells Optimization Engineer

WOG	water-oil-gas
WOL	weldolet
WOM	Worldwide Oilfield Machine, Inc.
WOO	wait on orders
WOPITS	workover pump in temperature survey
WOR	water oil ratio
WOW	wait on weather
WP	weather protected
WP	well pad
WP	working pressure
WPHY	wrought pipe high yield *(material grade designation from ASTM; author might not want it defined though)*
WPM	wellpad manifold (building)
WPO	Well Pad Operator
WPOM	Western Production Optimization Model
WPQ	Welder/Welding Operator Performance Qualification
WPQ	Welding Procedure Qualification
WPQR	Welding Procedure Qualification Record
WPQT	Welding Procedure Qualification Test
WPS	Welding Procedure Specification
WPS	well pad separator
WPWZ	Western Peripheral Wedge Zone
WRTA	wireless remote terminal access
WS	West Sak
WSA	Well Services Alliance
WSE	Written Scheme of Examination
WSL	Well Site Leader
WSO	water shut off
WSS	walking speed survey
WSS	Well Service Supervisor
WSW	west side waterflood
wt %	weight percent
Wt	weight
WW	well work
WWT	wastewater treatment

X

X (e.g., 5X)	magnification (power of)
X	horizontal offset distance

X0	neutral of transformer
XHHW	cross-linked high-heat water-resistant
XLS	spreadsheet
XT	Christmas tree
XXS	extra, extra, strong (standard pipe thickness)

Y

Y	zero-to-peak displacement of the pipeline motion, usually established at mid-span
ybp	years before present
yd	yard
yd^3	cubic yards
YPEAK	peak-to-peak displacement of the pipeline motion, usually established at mid-span.
yr	year
YRMS	RMS displacement of the pipeline motion, usually established at mid-span
YTD	year to date

Z

Z	pipe section modulus
ZI	zonal isolation
ZS	Zener (Shunt)

14.0   MEASUREMENT ABBREVIATIONS

These are measurement abbreviations many of my clients use.
Depending on how often they are used in the text, I might only use them
in tables and figures, and spell out in the text; it depends on the word.
For example, I always spell out foot or feet and inch or inches in the text,
but I do define first use and then use the abbreviation for square feet or
cubic feet. This is purely based on number of characters. Since the
abbreviation for "feet" is "ft" or at some companies "ft." I don't see the
point of using "ft." throughout, which is three characters, when the actual
word is only four. Just use your best judgment.

A

acre .... ac
acre-foot.. ac-ft
actual cubic feet per minute.. acfm

alternating current...AC
ampere .... A or amp
angstrom ....Å
ante meridiem (before noon) ....a.m.
atmosphere.. atm
atomic mass unit ....amu
atomic weight ....at wt

B

barrel.. bbl
barrels per day .... bpd
below ground surface...bgs
board foot..bd ft
boiling point.. bp
British thermal unit..Btu

C

calorie (small)..cal
calorie (large)..Cal
centimeter ....cm
centipoise.. cP

cubic centimeter .... cm^3 (cc for gas volume only)
cubic centimeter-second .... cm^3-sec
cubic foot.. ft^3
cubic feet per day ....cfd or ft^3/day
cubic feet per hour.. cf/h
cubic feet per minute .... cfm or ft^3/min
cubic feet per second .... cfs or ft^3/sec
cubic meter .... m^3
cubic yard ....cy
curie..Ci
cycles per minute..cpm
cycles per second... cps or Hz

D
decibel ....dB
decibel, A-weighted..dBA
degrees Celsius..°C
degrees Fahrenheit.. °F
degrees Kelvin...K
diameter..diam
direct current.. DC

E
electromagnetic force .... emf
electromagnetic unit ....emu
electron volt...eV
et alia (and others) ....et al.
et cetera ....etc.

F
foot .... ft
feet per minute... fpm or ft/min
feet per second..fps or ft/sec
foot-pound ....ft-lb

G
gallon...gal
gallons per acre per day ....gpad
gallons per day...gpd
gallons per minute .... gpm
gallons per second ....gps

grain .... gr
gram .... g
gram-square centimeter .... g-cm^2
gravitational constant..G

H
hertz ....Hz
horsepower .... hp
hour... hr
horizontal to vertical ....H:V

I
id est (that is) ....i.e.
inch .... in.
inside diameter..I.D.

J
joule ....J

K
kelvin (temperature unit) ....K
Kelvin (temperature scale)..K
kilo.. k

kilocycles per second (kilohertz)...kHz
kilocalorie...kcal
kiloelectron volt...keV
kilogram... kg
kilometer... km
kilovolt..kV
kilovolt ampere...kVA
kilowatt...kW
kilowatt-hour ....kWh

L
liter.. L

M
magnification (power of)... X (*e.g.*, 5X)
mean lower low water.. MLLW
mean low water..MLW
mean sea level..MSL

mega (million) .... M
megahertz .... MHz
megavolt .... MV
megawatt .... MW
melting point .... mp
meter .... m
metric ton .... metric ton or tonne
microgram .... µg
microgram per kilogram .... µg/kg (same as ppb)
microgram per liter .... µg/L (same as ppb)
microliter .... µL
micrometer .... µm
micromho .... µmho
micromolar .... µM or µM
micromoles .... µmol
micron (micrometer) .... µm
microsiemen .... µS
mile .... mi
milliequivalent .... meq
milligram .... mg
milligram per kilogram .... mg/kg (same as ppm)
milligram per liter .... mg/L (same as ppm)
milliliter .... ml (for liquid capacity; for gases, use cc)
millimeter .... mm
millimicron .... mµ
million gallons per day .... mgd
million electron volts .... MeV
million standard cubic feet per day .... mscfd
millivolt .... mv
milliwatt .... mw
minute .... min
molar .... M or M
molecular weight .... mol wt
mole percent .... mol %
month .... mo.

N
nanocurie .... nCi
normal (concentration) .... N or N

normal cubic meters .... Nm^3
ounce...oz
outside diameter..O.D.

P
page... p.
pages... pp.
parts per billion... ppb
parts per billion by volume.. ppbv
parts per million.. ppm
parts per million by volume.. ppmv
percent .... % (*in tables, spell out in text*)
post meridiem (after noon) .... p.m.
pound .... lb
pounds per cubic foot .... pcf or lb/ft^3
pounds per square foot .... psf or lb/ft^2
pounds per square inch ....psi
pounds per square inch, absolute.. psia
pounds per square inch gauge..psig

Q
quart.. qt

S
second.. sec or s
specific gravity ....sp gr
square centimeter..sq cm or cm^2
square feet.. sq ft or ft^2
standard cubic feet per minute..scfm
standard deviation.. SD
standard error of the mean ....SE

T
temperature (tables only)... temp.
thousand (kilo).. k
ton, metric... metric ton or tonne
tons per day... tpd

V
versus (tables only).. vs.
volt...V

volume per volume .... v/v
volume percent .... vol%

W

watt .... W
watt-hour .... W-hr
week .... wk
weight .... wt
weight per volume .... w/v
weight percent .... wt %

Y

yard .... yd
year .... yr
years before present .... ybp

ABOUT THE AUTHOR

Lori Jo Oswald is a freelance technical writer and technical editor who lives in Palmer, Alaska. She received her Ph.D. in English from the University of Oregon in 1994, and later earned a computer science degree. During graduate school, she began her career as a technical writer and editor, and has been writing and editing reports ever since. Additionally, she has taught English and Business Communications at Umpqua Community College, Lane Community College, and the University of Oregon, all in Oregon; Green River Community College in Washington; and the University of Alaska Anchorage. Her businesses include Wordsworth LLC, a technical editing company (wordsworthwriting.net) and Forms in Word (a document design and formatting company). She has also volunteered for humane societies for over 30 years.

Education-based Books by Lori Jo Oswald (available on www.amazon.com):

Children's Realistic Animal Fiction of Twentieth-Century North America

Priority on Learning: How School Districts and Schools Are Concentrating Their Scarce Resources on Academics

Quality Work Teams: Rationale and Implementation Guidelines

School-based Management: Rationale and Implementation Guidelines

Style Guide for Architectural, Engineering, Environmental, and Construction Firms

Style Guide for Oil Companies and Contractors

www.ingramcontent.com/pod-product-compliance
Lightning Source LLC
Chambersburg PA
CBHW060617290526
45793CB00001B/58